AMERICAN BUSINESS ABROAD

Origins and Development
of the Multinational Corporation

AMERICAN BUSINESS ABROAD

Origins and Development of the Multinational Corporation

Advisory Editor
STUART BRUCHEY

Associate Editor
ELEANOR BRUCHEY

Editorial Board
RAYMOND VERNON
MIRA WILKINS

See last pages of this volume for a complete list of titles

FOREIGN FINANCIAL CONTROL IN CHINA,

T[heodore] W. Overlach

ARNO PRESS
A New York Times Company
1976

Editorial Supervision: SHEILA MEHLMAN

———◆———

Reprint Edition 1976 by Arno Press Inc.

Reprinted from a copy in
  The Newark Public Library

AMERICAN BUSINESS ABROAD: Origins and
Development of the Multinational Corporation
ISBN for complete set: 0-405-09261-X
See last pages of this volume for titles.

Manufactured in the United States of America

———◆———

Library of Congress Cataloging in Publication Data
Overlach, Theodore William, 1887-
    Foreign financial control in China.

    (American business abroad)
    Reprint of the 1919 ed. published by Macmillan, New
York.
    1. China--Economic conditions--1912-1949. 2. Fi-
nance--China. 3. China--Foreign relations. I. Title.
II. Series.
HC427.08 1976   332.6'73'0951   76-5027
ISBN 0-405-09293-8

FOREIGN FINANCIAL CONTROL
IN CHINA

FOREIGN FINANCIAL CONTROL IN CHINA

BY

T. W. OVERLACH

New York
THE MACMILLAN COMPANY
1919

TO

THE MEMORY OF
WILLARD D. STRAIGHT

CONTENTS

THEORETICAL INTRODUCTION

CHAPTER I

CHAPTER II

CHAPTER III

CHAPTER IV

CHAPTER V

CONTENTS

CHAPTER VIII PAGE

THEORETICAL INTRODUCTION

WITH the conclusion of the Chino-Japanese War in 1895, a new era opened in the Far East, an era of rapid encroachment on China by powerful western nations and by Japan. These powers secured strategic bases on Chinese territory and sought to control certain parts of the Empire through the medium of railways. Railway concessions, and to some extent public loans, were the instruments by which the foreign powers advanced and carried out their policies. The obvious tendency of foreign ambitions at this time in regard to railway enterprise was to secure a monopoly of rights within socalled " spheres of interest," and as far as possible to exclude Chinese as well as other foreigners not only from securing concessions but also from any share in the control or management of those railways that were to be constructed in their respective spheres.

Though at first sight political, and fought by diplomacy, the struggle for foreign control in China was not less one of international financial interests, contending for the exploitation of new opportunities for investment. Foreign capital was attracted by the great profits to be

gained from the impending industrial revolution of China.
In order to eliminate financial competition of other nations or to counteract political moves on the part of other
governments, if such were destined to be harmful to its
own expansion, foreign finance often solicited, and freely
received, diplomatic protection. With a protection and
promotion of foreign enterprise several governments
combined the furtherance of national ambitions of a
more or less political character. All banks and syndicates in charge of the railways and loans became more
and more generally recognized as indispensable means to
the political and commercial ends of their respective governments. The struggle for foreign control in China
has accordingly been marked by a most singular and dis-
tinguishing feature, namely, the closest possible coöperation between foreign finance and foreign policy. The
period was one of " conquest by railroad and bank."

The tenacious determination on the part of several
powers to control their respective spheres to the greatest
possible exclusion of their competitors not only tended to
prejudice China's integrity but also the full and free enjoyment of the treaty rights of others. Though protesting vehemently and professing adherence to the " open
door " doctrine nations viewed, nevertheless, with jealousy the preserves seized by others. They were driven
to bitter diplomatic strife over each new prospective
" sphere." In short, the tremendous pressure of modern

imperialism coupled with modern capitalistic enterprise was, in China as elsewhere on earth, a constant menace to peace; and a continued application of imperialistic policies to exclusively national ends might again make for war, as soon as the present conflict is over. For China will unquestionably become once more one of the principal centers of world politics, in which Great Britain, Russia, France, Germany, Japan, and the United States are concerned.

But whatever the future relations of these nations in reference to China may be, it would appear that a clearer vision in international affairs would go far towards preventing further hostilities, namely, if each nation, with unprejudiced mind, would candidly consider the claims of an opponent as well as its own and would seek to strike a fair balance by mutual concession.   Such is at least what we propose to do in the following modest contribution to the study of recent and present day financial and political activities of foreign powers in China. We shall adopt a sympathetic view and attitude towards all the powers concerned, trying to give justice to each, instead of seeing things through the colored glasses of national ambitions. To offer a solution, to give suggestions or to pass judgment can obviously not fall within the scope of our investigation. We merely aim to give a comparative and scientific account of what we consider the most tangible and concrete problem of the otherwise so elusive Far

Eastern Question, namely, the problem of "Foreign Financial Control in China."

Before we can offer a definite program for our investigation we shall have to define our task more clearly. To that end it will be necessary to analyze certain theoretical phrases in their application to our problem and to reduce them to their true meanings. And we shall not be held to anticipate unduly if we define, at the outset, terms which will constantly reappear, although detailed illustrations will as a matter of course have to be reserved for their proper places.

The principal phrases which we have in mind are: "spheres of interest," "spheres of influence," "independence," "open door," "concessions," and "control."

One thing common to all these terms is their flexibility; for they have been used with the greatest latitude of meaning and have been applied to a great variety of relations; but through all their uses run certain special characteristics which may be determined with a fair degree of accuracy.[1] The most confusing terms, often used interchangeably even in theoretical literature,[2] are "spheres of interest" and "spheres of influence." A "sphere of interest" is officially earmarked by non-aliena-

---

[1] See P. S. Reinsch, "Colonial Government," page 103.

[2] W. E. Hall and L. Oppenheim, both of whom will be quoted below, in their treatises on International Law, fail to distinguish clearly between the two phrases, apparently only having conditions in Africa in mind. See Hall, pages 129 to 131, and Oppenheim, Vol. I, page 297.

tion declarations extracted from the Chinese Government and officially created by an agreement between two powers. It refers to an area frequently adjacent to a possession or a protected or leased territory within which area the foreign power claims the primary right of economic exploitation.[3] Its essential element is a negative one; namely, the term expresses the principle that no other power except the one in whose favor the "sphere of interest" exists shall be permitted to acquire concessions or to exert any control or influence whatsoever — not to speak about military occupation — at the same time giving the privileged power a monopoly of the right to seek concessions.[4] This privilege, however, does by no means entitle its holder to any positive exercise of "influence" within the sphere which would change the "sphere of interest" into a "sphere of influence." For the latter term, which never has been used officially, as far as China is concerned, suggests a certain degree of authority or control, either financial or political, exercised by a foreign power within a certain territory.

Political control, however, has to stop short of changing the "sphere of influence" into a protectorate.

---

[3] Foreign "spheres" in China are, legally, only economic spheres in contrast to the political spheres of Africa.

[4] See Reinsch, page 103. Otto Köbner, "Kolonialpolitik," page 14: "Streng rechtlich betrachtet liegt also nur ein pactum de excludendo alium vor. . . . Erfolgt von Seiten einer dritten Macht ein Widerspruch nicht, so ist rechtlich ein ius excludendi alios, allen fremden Mächten gegenüber entstanden."

Though eventual occupation may be contemplated, the region has "not actually been so reduced into control that the minimum of the powers which are implied in a protectorate can be exercised with tolerable regularity." [5]

As long as control consists merely of a legitimate protection of the financier, subject to agreements of an exclusively financial nature, no objection can be raised by anybody. But as soon as the exercise of a reasonable financial control changes into the exercise of an administrative control or an assumption of territorial supremacy by a foreign power, without any sanction on the side of the Chinese, such control would seriously menace the supreme sovereign authority, in other words, the independence, of China. For one of the marks of an independent state is that "it is independent of external control." [6] "In the interest of the territorial supremacy of other states, a state is not allowed to send its troops . . . or its police forces into . . . foreign territory, or to exercise an act of administration or jurisdiction on foreign territory without permission." [7]

The wielding of a political control would also be violating the socalled "open door" policy. For this policy aims to be an instrument for the maintenance of the integrity of China and the preservation of an "equal oppor-

[5] See W. E. Hall, "International Law," page 129.
[6] See Hall, op cit., page 17.
[7] See L. Oppenheim, "International Law," Vol. I, page 179.

tunity for all." It is mainly directed against the assumption of an undue administrative control or territorial supremacy within a " sphere." It is, however, not explicitly opposed to the policy of " spheres of interest," and not necessarily to the " sphere of influence " as long as influence means financial control within reasonable bounds. Indeed, the " open door " principle recognizes the " vested rights " and " special interests " within such spheres as long as a certain amount of opportunity for others is preserved, that is, as long as the Chinese treaty tariff is indiscriminately applied, as long as treaty ports are kept open and as long as no harbor dues or railroad charges are levied higher than those imposed upon subjects of the country in whose favor the " sphere " exists. The principle is also more or less opposed to the acquisition of a monopoly in the supply of railway materials and rolling stock.

To return to the term " sphere of interest ": The interests have invariably taken the form of the socalled railroad " concessions." The term concession has been as loosely applied as the other phrases. Railroad concessions are agreements, conferring on the foreigner certain rights of financing, building and managing of railroads. In several cases where the railroad grants have been made under conditions which deprive China of almost all control and profit in the several undertakings, and which lead to political control and therefore prejudice her sovereign rights within the " sphere," the term " cession " might be more appropriate than " concession." In many cases the " concessions," that is, the railroad agreements, are simply in the nature of underwriting contracts. In no instance have the Chinese parted with the ultimate property in the railways.

The grantor of the railway concessions as well as the principal claimant of capital was the Chinese Government. But while to strong and reliable governments money is entrusted unconditionally, China's political insecurity, together with her financial inexperience, forced the foreign financier to maintain a great amount of control over his investments. The principal feature of all railroad agreements then are the " control " clauses, and the word " control " in this connection is being used " to denote certain financial safeguards for the protection of loan funds " in the interest of the owners and the bondholders.[8] These safeguards either consist of a first mortgage upon the railway if owned by the Chinese Government and in a certain share in the management of the line in order to prevent fraud and to secure efficiency and an adequate return, since the lenders usually are entitled to a share in the profits of the line. Or " control " means direct management by the foreign owners, if the railway is nominally a private foreign and Chinese joint stock

---

[8] The quotations in the definition of control have been taken from W. D. Straight, " Recent Developments in China," page 131.

company in which the Chinese in the natural course of things had but little share.

The word " control " similarly refers to loans, in which connection it signifies certain " guarantees against improper loan fund expenditure," and secures principal and interest by some special hypothecation and the supervision or management thereof — as, for instance, when the revenue of customs, taxes, or some monopoly is pledged.

Furthermore has the word " control," though inaccurately, been used in connection with certain monopolies, which interest us only secondarily. On the one hand have the contracting bankers occasionally " controlled " the supply of railway materials and rolling stock by stipulating that such were to be purchased from the manufacturers of their respective countries. On the other hand did the bankers through national or international monopolistic syndicates attempt to " control " the money supply to China.

The main points we now mean to emphasize, are:

First, that the " control " clauses embodied in the several concessions as well as loan agreements are nominally of a financial character. All railways and loans are nominally, as far as foreigners are concerned, financed, managed, or controlled by private citizens, and the control provisions constitute nothing else but foreign expert supervision or management to secure adequate profits. That is to say: the provisions confer legally upon the foreigner no rights to political control.

Secondly, that the " sphere of interest " policy and the agreements referring thereto do likewise not confer upon the privileged power any rights to political control. For China had not the slightest intention of selling its sovereign rights within said spheres.

Thirdly, that the several control provisions vary considerably as to character and degree since they reflect the tendencies of the Far Eastern policies of foreign powers which either represent the results of economic pressure or serve as incidents in a larger policy of national imperialism. It is important, in this connection, to bear in mind, that concessions and loan contracts have been negotiated not only by bankers who acted as politico-financial agents of their governments but also by diplomats directly. And it will be observed that, whereas it was the aim of the one power to insist upon " adequate control " for economic purposes and incidentally to China's interest, it was the aim of the other power to control railways or loans for more or less political purposes and against China's interests. The control provisions therefore often tended to evade, by practices which are difficult to trace definitely, the principle of equal opportunity, and to undermine China's sovereignty. In other words, foreign control in China is nominally purely financial, and if political, it is an undue extension of financial control by means of a peculiar wording and an arbitrary interpretation of the control clauses embodied in the different railroad and loan agreements.

It might be objected here that certain powers have exercised and still exercise control upon other premises than railroad or loan agreements. It is one of the aims of our investigation to show that this is not the case,— with the exception of the Maritime Customs Service in its original form.[9] True enough, several powers have controlled Chinese territory by military force. Such control, however, has always remained a temporary measure. Control as we understand it, is of a permanent nature. Neither must " foreign control " be confused with the sovereign rights enjoyed by foreign powers within " leased territories," nor with the rights of extraterritoriality, nor with foreign administration of international settlements. In the first two cases China has explicitly ceded certain sovereign rights, and the third case is practically nothing but an extension of the right of extraterritoriality. Foreign " control " is exercised where no sovereign rights have been ceded. If we entitle this book " Foreign Financial Control in China " we do so firstly to avoid any possible confusion, and secondly to indicate the sources as well as the raison d'être of foreign " control."

By too many distinctions at the outset, however, we

[9] See Chapter I.

might anticipate certain results of our investigation. The advantages and justification of narrowing down the vast field of foreign finance and foreign policies in China to a more concrete question of foreign financial control will, we trust, become clearer when the proceedings and problems which have been touched upon are analyzed and narrated in detail. We shall consider these by treating each foreign power individually, although such treatment may involve repetition in certain particulars, seeing that the several policies are occasionally closely connected. In order to understand fully the character and degree of foreign control and the policies and operating causes underlying it, we shall have to give a comprehensive knowledge of past and existing affairs, conditions, and problems. The method of our investigation therefore must be mainly historical. By considering the vastness of the field, the thesis can only aim at a brief analysis and interpretation of history, based upon the most important documents and utterances of authorities and writers such as are enumerated in the Bibliography. Many important events which have no direct bearing upon the subject will have to be left unmentioned. Likewise will many of the numerous railways and loans, either contracted or projected, have to be left undiscussed. For our purposes it will be sufficient to consider only the more important contracts and agreements.

The main investigation is to be preceded by a general

historical introduction, which makes no claim to scientific value whatsoever. In this chapter we merely intend to set the stage, so to speak. The arrangement of the chapters which then follow will not be strictly chronological but rather chronological, subject to geographical and historical conditions. A separate chapter is to be devoted to international control, while in the conclusion some reflections will be made. A word has to be said about the spelling of Chinese names. The writer has not adopted a uniform system, but has quoted names as he found them printed. The inconsistency in spelling them is due to the fact that each author spells Chinese names as he pleases. The majority of these conform to Giles' system or to common usage.

In concluding our introductory remarks we venture to believe that the subject demands the treatment which we have outlined, and that it will be found both logical and convenient.

FOREIGN FINANCIAL CONTROL IN CHINA

CHAPTER I

FOREIGN RELATIONS WITH CHINA BEFORE 1895

CHINA's recent and present day international relations will be better understood on the basis of a knowledge of the development of these relations during the nineteenth century. Of the literature available on this period [1] we have principally followed the two admirable accounts of Sargent, " Anglo-Chinese Commerce and Diplomacy," and Morse, " The International Relations of the Chinese Empire "; and since we can dwell upon the nineteenth century previous to 1895 only in an introductory way, we shall content ourselves with a brief summary of the two books, supported by references to official documents and by a few other quotations.

China has been opened by England to intercourse with the modern world. The early history of British relations with China is to all practical purposes the history of the East India Company, which made the project of opening up a trade with China an integral part of her

[1] See Bibliography, Section VI.

I

policy. The great bulk of the capital required for the trade with the East was invested in ships and goods and in a few trading stations in fixed establishments abroad. The Company's station in China was the " factory " at Canton where she enjoyed a monopoly granted to her by Great Britain and special privileges obtained from China. This twofold advantage enabled the Company to maintain her commercial predominance of the Chinese trade intact throughout the various vicissitudes of its fortunes and in spite of the modifications introduced at successive intervals of the charter. The excellent responsible organization gave her the further advantage of stability in dealing with the Hong merchants and Chinese officials. The latter in their intercourse with foreigners concerned themselves only with two points: the revenue and taxes imposed arbitrarily to be collected, and the orderly behavior of the traders. As intermediary in all things between the Chinese officials and the foreigners they instituted the Hong, which was a body of merchants numbering from two to eleven. The Hong was responsible to the government for the good behavior of the foreigners, and for the customs duties on the whole trade, including that of outside or unprivileged merchants. The responsibility of the Hong merchants was more than nominal. No foreign ship was allowed to trade until one of their body had become security for the good behavior of the crew. Those strict regulations served the purpose of restricting the energetic foreigner to only such intercourse as could be carried on under official supervision. The monopoly system of the Hong was eminently calculated to attain this end. The functions of the Hong were thus diplomatic or political as well as commercial. In the former capacity they acted as a convenient barrier between the degraded " barbarian " and official pride; in the latter they were useful as a fairly safe and regular means of filling official coffers.

In their dealings with the Hong and the officials, the Company, as the only representative foreign body, was compelled by its traditions to champion the cause of foreigners in general and it was only at the close of the eighteenth century that the British Government began to take official intercourse in its own hands. This first step was the embassy of Lord Macartney, sent out both on behalf of the East India Company, and in order to improve the general relations between the two nations. It was pointed out to Macartney that, though the English were more numerous than other foreigners at Canton, they had hitherto had no official communication with the Chinese Government, and that it was the duty of the Sovereign to take up the matter and defend the interests of his subjects. Here is the beginning of a trouble which required a century for its settlement. It was thought that the local rather than the Imperial officials were responsible for the vexatious restrictions on intercourse with

foreigners, and subsequent diplomatic history is largely
concerned with attempts to establish direct relations with,
and wring concessions from, the Chinese Government.
The main questions which were destined to be fought out
in the nineteenth century were the legal control over foreigners and the conditions under which commercial intercourse was to be allowed.

With the beginning of the nineteenth century, this
intercourse had become more and more difficult. The
number of foreigners resorting annually to Canton had
greatly increased; disturbances were frequent, the anti-
foreign feeling became more clearly marked, and there
was undoubtedly, on the part of the Chinese, a distinct
intention to restrict as far as possible the existing privileges of foreigners. With the appearance of numerous
private traders the commercial importance of the East
India Company began to decline and the profits which so
far had been satisfactory began to diminish. In view of
these commercial and political difficulties and of the growing hostility of the Chinese, the position of the Company
was becoming critical. A final attempt to improve her
relations with China by invoking the aid of the State
and sending out the embassy of Lord Amherst in 1816
with the hope that the establishment of direct relations
between the two governments might lead to better trade
conditions generally, also proved a failure. In consequence of all this, the monopoly of the Company was

abolished in 1833, owing especially to a large force behind Parliament, both of traders and theorists, who advocated open trade on various grounds.

Simultaneously with the abolishment of the monopoly, other orders in Council provided regulations for future relations.[2] Three " superintendents " were contemplated to present British authority. The orders also give power to the Crown to create a Court of Justice with criminal and admiralty jurisdiction at Canton and to appoint one of the superintendents to be the officer to hold such a court. Here we have the formal opening of British relations with China. The instructions by Lord Palmerston to Lord Napier and his colleagues, as the first superintendents, throw considerable light on the ideas and policy of the Home Government.[3] The superintendents were enjoined to watch over trade generally and to adjust disputes between British subjects and Chinese or foreigners. In doing so they had to avoid irritating Chinese officials and above all impress on British subjects the duty of conforming to the laws and usages of the Chinese Empire. Lord Napier was directed to ascertain how far it might be possible to extend trade to other parts of China and to seek for the best means of establishing direct relations with China. There is evident in

[2] See "Additional Papers Relating to China," 1840, Vol. XXXVI.
[3] See "Correspondence Relating to China," 1840, Vol. XXXVI, No. 2.

these instructions an attempt to give effect to the aspirations of the British mercantile community towards a wider trade based on more secure conditions than the custom of the Company.

The Chinese were well aware of the radical difference between these new officials and their predecessors, and they did all in their power to counteract the British policy. Thus Napier's mission was unsatisfactory. It then became clear that nothing had been gained by the removal of the East India Company; on the contrary the Chinese were attempting further restrictions and continued to refuse acknowledgment of the Government emissaries. However, on February 2nd, 1837, the Chinese policy underwent a little change, when an Imperial Edict gave the required permission for admittance to Canton to Superintendent Elliott as comptroller, who after months of negotiations was successful in really establishing his official position after having boldly informed the viceroy of his appointment to the station of the " Chief English authority in China." [4] His admission marks a new chapter in the history of English commercial relations with China. The English abandoned the quiescent policy of the earlier times and showed determination. The first result of the new policy was the Opium War, during which the British took permanent possession of Hong-

4 See " Correspondence Relating to China," 1840, Vol. XXXVI, pages 142 ff.

kong. The war was concluded by the treaty of Nanking of August 29th, 1842.[5]

Its enactments are simple in the extreme — they are:

1. The conclusion of a lasting peace between China and Great Britain.

2. The payment of an indemnity of $21,000,000 by China to England: $3,000,000 to settle Hong debts, $12,-000,000 to cover expenses, and $6,000,000 as opium compensation.

3. The opening of Amoy, Canton, Fuchow, Ningpo, and Shanghai to British trade.

4. The cession of the island of Hongkong to England.

5. The provision for free transit of goods after payment of the tariff and a fixed transit duty.

Opium was the immediate cause of the war. The Chinese tried to stop opium smuggling, which was strongly supported by the Indian Government. India was profiting enormously by the trade and did not wish to discontinue it. When the Chinese stopped it they put themselves in the wrong. Yet opium was not the principal reason for hostilities. A contemporary conception of the significance of the Opium War is given by John Quincy Adams in an address before the Massachusetts Historical Society, November 22nd, 1841, on the subject of " The War between England and China."

[5] See W. F. Mayers, " Treaties Between the Empire of China and Foreign Powers," page 1.

" The justice of the cause between the two parties,—which has the righteous cause? You have perhaps been surprised to hear me answer, Britain. Britain has the righteous cause. But to prove it, I have been obliged to show that the opium question is not the cause of the war. My demonstration is not yet complete. The cause of the war is the kowtow! — the arrogant and insupportable pretension of China that she will hold commercial intercourse with the rest of mankind, not upon terms of equal reciprocity, but upon the insulting and degrading forms of lord and vassal." [6]   " In fact the direct cause of the war was the growing sense of the need for better protection to life and property, though behind this was the ground cause of the need for better relations generally." [7]   The Treaty of Nanking, then, intended to settle the disputes between the mandarins and the British traders and it was to be the charter of commercial rights in China, acknowledging for the first time in history, the existence of a Western Power on an equality with the Celestial Empire: For Article I stipulates that the respective subjects " shall enjoy full security and protection for their persons and property within the dominions of the other," while according to Article II Great Britain " will appoint Super-

[6] Boston *Evening Transcript*, Wednesday, Nov. 24, 1841, quoting the transactions of the Massachusetts Historical Society of Nov. 22, 1841.
[7] See H. B. Morse, " The Trade and Administration of China," page 36.

intendents or Consular Officers, to reside at each of the
above-named cities or towns, to be the medium of communication between the Chinese authorities and the
merchants."

But when England accepted the treaty in final settlement of the annoyances which had led to the war of
1839, she had reckoned without her host. Owing to the
fact that the Chinese were not permitted by a Christian
nation to abolish the infamous opium traffic because it
was a very lucrative one, and owing to the humiliation
of their defeat and of the Treaty of Nanking, which has
" inflicted a deep wound in the pride, but by no means
altered the policy of the Chinese Government," [8] and last,
but not least, owing to the conservative and even stub-
born disinclination on the side of the Chinese to treat
other nations on terms of equality, relations between
China and other Powers, and especially with Great Britain, continued unstable. The Chinese view of the treaty
was in marked contrast to its terms. China had signed
it reluctantly and merely to stop the incursions of the
British in her realms, and, having obtained her aim, she
made no attempt to abide by its provisions. Thus the
period following the Treaty was filled with further disturbances and difficulties in the relations, the principal
complaint being that charges still were suddenly and

[8] See Alexis Krausse, " The Far East," page 36.

arbitrarily imposed by the provincial officials in spite of the treaty stipulations.

But on the other hand, the reports and opinions of consuls drawn up for the benefit of Lord Elgin show plainly that many elements of disturbance were also to be found within the European settlements, and that in the matter of observance of treaties the Chinese were far from being the only offenders.[9]

To quote Sargent [10]: " Foreign merchants, in direct custom-house relations with Chinese authorities, all more or less venal and corrupt, launched into a wholesale system of smuggling and fraudulent devices for the evasion of duties. Contempt for all Chinese authority, and disregard of inherent rights, habitual infraction of treaty stipulations, licence and violence wherever the offscum of the European nations found access, and peaceable people to plunder — such were the first-fruits of this important concession; and time only served to increase their growth."

Conditions soon pointed to another armed interference in which the French joined hands with the English, while Russia and the United States abstained strictly from any hostile steps, using moral suasion alone. The result of the interference was the Treaty of Tientsin, which

[9] Correspondence relating to Earl of Elgin's special mission to China, 1857 to 1859, " China," 1859, Vol. XXXIII, No. 1.
[10] Sargent, op. cit., page 103.

was signed with China on the 26th of June, 1858, by Lord Elgin in connection with representatives of France.[11] This treaty strengthens that previously arranged at Nanking, and supplies several omissions in the former. It serves as the ultimate basis of foreign relations with China and therefore merits a close examination. The most important novelty is put in the forefront of the document. Article 2 provides for the sending of an ambassador to the court of Peking with all the usual privileges of such ministers and the dispatch of a similar representative from China to London. He may come and go at pleasure; his letters are to be inviolable; he may communicate with a high official on terms of equality, and shall not be called on to perform " any ceremony derogatory to him as representing the Sovereign of an independent nation." By this clause, China is compelled, once and for all, to surrender her formal claim of superiority over western nations, which was one of the most cherished principles of the traditional policy of the Empire. Next in importance to the position of the British representative comes the fuller recognition of the principle of extraterritoriality. Referring to the latter Morse writes,[12] " English . . . were not molested so long as they were law-abiding, but law-abiding in the sense of the law of China. It was irksome to them to have no

[11] See Mayers op. cit., page 11.
[12] See Morse, " Trade and Administration of China," page 179.

lawyer to instruct them in the law of the land, to have no fixed and certain law to appeal to, to be doubtful of the application of the law to any particular case, and to have no doubt whatever on the course likely to be followed by the administrators of the law." While the Treaty of Nanking made consuls the " medium of communication between Chinese authorities and the merchants," and while the supplementary treaty of Hoomunchae [13] merely contained provisions for extradition, and regulations regarding the punishment of English criminals, Article XV of the Treaty of Tientsin establishes the principle of extraterritoriality as far as British subjects only are concerned: " All questions in regard to rights, whether of property or persons, arising between British subjects, shall be subject to the jurisdiction of the British authorities." The principle of extraterritoriality was more clearly expressed and expanded in the Chefoo Convention of 1876,[14] between Great Britain and China, providing for mixed jurisdiction between English and Chinese, and again in the American Supplemental Treaty of Peking of 1880:[15] In the latter, Article IV reads as follows: —

" When controversies arise in the Chinese Empire between citizens of the United States and subjects of His Imperial Majesty, which need to be examined and de-

[13] See Mayers, op. cit., page 5.
[14] See Mayers, op, cit., page 44.
[15] See Malloy, " Treaties Between U. S. and Other Powers," Vol. I, pages 239 ff.

cided by the public officers of the two nations, it is agreed between the Governments of the United States and China that such cases shall be tried by the proper official of the nationality of the defendant. The properly authorized official of the plaintiff's nationality shall be freely permitted to attend the trial, and shall be treated with the courtesy due to his position. He shall be granted all proper facilities for watching the proceedings in the interests of justice. If he so desires, he shall have the right to present, to examine, and to cross-examine witnesses. If he is dissatisfied with the proceedings he shall be permitted to protest against them in detail. The law administered will be the law of the nationality of the officer trying the case."

Articles IX–XI of the Treaty of Tientsin contain the new concessions. British subjects may travel for pleasure or trade to all parts of the interior, under passports issued by their Consuls, and countersigned by the local authorities. Newchwang, Tangchow, Taiwan, Swatow, and Kiungchow are opened as new treaty ports, where foreigners are privileged to establish consulates and foreign merchants are permitted to live and trade. The new area thus provided for British enterprise was greatly extended by the opening of the Yangtsze to British merchant ships.

Finally Article XXVIII deals with the vexed question of inland transit duties. At all the treaty ports there are levied dues and duties on the trade according to a tariff settled by both parties. Goods were exempted from all further taxation on movement by one initial payment, except that the goods go "inland" to a place which is not a treaty port, where the bale is liable to the taxation which is levied in China on all movement of commodities not exempted by "special privilege." This is the one reason underlying the constant demand for the opening of new treaty ports, with all the expense for administrative work imposed on China, and for the enforcement of extraterritorial rights. This Article XXVIII does away with the arbitrary imposition by provincial authorities of transit duties, so much complained of by British merchants, and stipulates a single transit charge to be declared by the collector of duties and to be levied at the first barrier or at the landing port. The charge is to be as near as possible 2½ ad valorem. Hereafter goods are exempt from all further inland charges whatsoever.

Between the signature of the treaty and its ratification there was again a period of armed conflict, illustrating the reluctance of the Central Government. The Convention of Peking finally signed the treaty on October 24, 1860, a few days after the English and French Allies had found it necessary to give the Chinese a severe lesson in destroying the summer palace.

Treaties similar to the British treaty were immediately afterwards concluded by all the important powers.

The political history of the next few years is largely taken up with the difficulties incidental to the execution of the terms of the treaties. The governments standing behind the two contesting parties, the Chinese officials and the merchants, seemed to be disposed for a time to settle their differences by diplomacy rather than by force. The main step in that direction taken by China was the foundation of the Tsungli Yamen, or Board of Foreign Affairs, a product of the moderate party of Prince Kung. Having thus to deal with a responsible central body the English decided not to tolerate local pressure any longer and tried to induce the Chinese to adopt western ideas as to the subordination of local to central authority. The strengthening of central authority as against provincial authority would have been to China's own interests, since local officials were not willing to surrender revenue collected for the benefit of the Chinese Government, which was in need of resources to cope with the Taiping rebellion. In this connection the English helped China not only to strengthen centralization, but they also sent military aid to quell the Taiping rising, which at one moment threatened to overwhelm the whole country and to depose the Manchu dynasty. Thus the British Government committed itself definitely by this assistance rendered to the upholding of the dynasty and to the protection of the Empire's integrity.

In spite of all this friendly assistance, however, the attitude of the Chinese underwent no material change. Internal disorder and corruption seriously affected the execution of the treaties; the transit system continued to be totally inefficient and unsatisfactory. The internal administration of China was hopelessly corrupt; military and civil organization were in confusion; the Empire, without rail or telegraph, with its capital in the far north, was too vast for effective centralized government. Reorganization, indeed, was greatly needed everywhere. The only thing accomplished in that line was the reformation of the customs system on western lines, when native talents and methods were inadequate for dealing with the complicated conditions introduced by the Treaty of Tientsin.

The formation of the "foreign customs," says Morse,[16] " was laid in the necessities of the Chinese Government and not in any demand by the foreign merchant that an improved revenue service should be provided for them." The system grew out of the voluntary collection of customs established in Shanghai during the Taiping rebellion. It was ever more enlarged and Rule 10 of the Agreement of the Tariff Commission of 1858 laid the foundation for the appointment of a foreign Inspector-

[16] See Morse's "Trade and Administration," page 366.

ate.[17] In 1863 Mr.— later Sir — Robert Hart was appointed Inspector General and brought the system to its highest possible efficiency, thus benefiting the Chinese as well as foreign creditors: for the Chinese Maritime Customs were to serve as securities for loans, to which we shall have occasion to refer later.

All further attempts on the European side at reorganization and the attempts to carry out the different treaty stipulations and the conventions for treaty revisions proved to be without any result. The Chinese were not only not prepared to make any further concessions but they also desired a great deal to be altered. The cardinal points of Chinese policy were brought to light at the Convention of 1869.[18] These were — the total prohibition of opium, the restriction of missionaries from inland residence, and the abolition of the principle of extraterritoriality. They amounted to the recovery of the greater part of that liberty which had been wrested from the Court of Peking in the various treaties. Chinese opposition was reënforced by the extravagant demands of the British merchants. The latter insisted upon the most sweeping changes, but were not disposed to concede anything. Indeed, their presence in China was not based on the desire to further the welfare of the Chinese but on their own benefit. And that in the treatment of China

17 See Mayers, op. cit., page 31.
18 See Mayers, op. cit., page 37.

by the foreigner much remained to be desired was amply illustrated by the plea of Burlingame in his famous mission on behalf of the Chinese Government.

The demands of the merchants were not only prompted by an unsatisfactory state of affairs in China, but they also reflected unsatisfactory trade results. For a quarter of a century after the passing of the East India Company, the British had cherished the idea that the Chinese Empire, once successfully opened to trade, would offer a vast field of lucrative opportunities for British merchants. The several wars and following treaties were deliberately undertaken for the development and protection of that field. Yet the renewed activities of trade as shown after the treaties of Nanking and Tientsin, and the extension of the markets by the addition of new treaty ports proved to be of little advantage to the foreign mercantile community in China. The possibilities of the trade and the opening of the Suez Canal had attracted large numbers of traders with small capital or credit, while the more responsible merchant, in anticipation of lower profits on each transaction, was naturally disposed to enlarge the scope of his operations by way of compensation. The result was an artificial expansion of business, greatly to the detriment of the merchants, but to the advantage perhaps of the British consumer and manufacturer and certainly greatly to the profit of the Chinese producer and merchant. These exploited to the full the competition among foreign buyers, who were helpless in the hands of the native dealer, since the latter was enabled by his excellent gild organization to maintain a strong control over the local markets and to keep up prices.[19] The control of the whole trade was fast getting into the hands of natives, last not least, through the foreigner's ignorance of language, while the foreigner began to decline to the position of a mere agent, and profits and influence dwindled together. The Chinese evidently were already discovering that there are other means than riot and open opposition for the ousting of the foreigner,— means that cannot be touched by force or treaty.

The increase of trade, furthermore, depended on the expansion of the area and population open to British trade rather than on the increased use of English goods. "If we consider the vastness of the native population within reach of our goods at the opening of the trade, we are forced to the conclusion that we were no nearer capturing the native markets, in the sense of supplying the everyday needs of the masses, in 1884 than in 1834. . . . The economic self-sufficiency of China was perhaps the most formidable barrier which we had as yet encountered in our career of industrial and commercial expansion." [20]

[19] See Schumacher, "Weltwirtschaftliche Studien," pages 430 ff. in: "Die Organisation des Fremdhandels in China."
[20] Sargeant, op. cit., pages 224, 225.

Looking back over the whole history of foreign relations with China since the abolition of the East India Company's trading monopoly, a few marked results clearly stand out: The most satisfactory result was the establishment of foreign financial control over the maritime customs service, which, however, should prove of greatest value and service at a later period and which will be duly referred to at the proper occasion. Furthermore, the principle of extraterritoriality was introduced in China. Though it had proved absolutely necessary for the protection of the foreigner, it put a stigma of inferiority on the Chinese which is evident in all further dealings between China and the foreign powers. It reversed the position of China which formerly was one of overbearance and contempt for the " barbarian." But treaties could neither alter national feelings and long-established customs, nor could they strengthen the inherent weakness of the Manchu administration and official corruption. Truly enough, tolerable conditions for commercial intercourse were established. Nevertheless, the Chinese trade, upon which great hopes had been founded, remained comparatively insignficant and unsatisfactory considering the sacrifices and risks incurred to develop it; while the experience revealed that it is impossible to create that trade by force of pressure or by treaties. Indeed, Europe used only a moderate amount of pressure in imposing its own will upon the Chinese Empire, as Morse in a summary of the " Period of Conflict " [21] emphasizes: " In time the world, East and West, will recognize that the West has exercised great restraint and shown a wise moderation in reaping the fruits of victory, and that the restrictions imposed on Chinese sovereignty were only those rendered indispensable by the inefficiency and corruption of the mandarinate of the Empire; but this was a lesson for future years; now, as the result of three wars, the Chinese learned, and they accepted as their law, that, whereas formerly it was China which dictated the conditions under which international relations were to be maintained, now it was the Western nations which imposed their will on China."

The policy adopted by the British Government following the Treaty of Tientsin was one of non-interference. It was found advisable to consolidate what was already gained, and for the future to trust to patient negotiation and moral influence. A reaction of discouragement had set in, which found its expression in a policy of laisser-faire adopted by the Home Government after the removal of Lord Palmerston from the Foreign Office. This policy also reflected a belief in China's ability ultimately to set her own house in order and a desire to be on friendly terms with other nations and to avoid any causes of friction.

In accordance with the laissez-faire and free-trade

[21] See Morse, " International Relations," page 617.

principles England was ready, after having obtained new outlets for trade and other privileges, to share them with other nations. Thus her acquisition of trade facilities was followed by the conclusion of similar treaties between China and other Powers. Britain had solved the problem of the conditions most favorable to national prosperity in her way, believing that open competition was the best condition for ensuring such prosperity. Wherever free-trade existed it meant British preponderance; and the predominance of England in China was admitted on all hands. Consequently, Great Britain did not attain exclusive privileges for the benefit of her trade and she strove by means of the "most favored nation" clause only to enjoy such privileges as have been accorded to other nations and no more. And she also was willing to refrain from the exaction of further privileges.

Thus her policy, however, had to undergo a moderation as soon as other countries began to seek special advantages at the expense of their competitors and of China. French aggrandizement in Tongking, and the declaration of a protectorate over Annam were followed by the Franco-Chinese Treaty of Tientsin, in June, 1885, which seriously affected British interests in setting up differential duties in favor of France and in defiance of English treaty rights.[22]

[22] See Mayers, op, cit., page 239.

The British Government could not view without concern the prospect of differential treatment for French goods entering China by way of the land frontier, and the danger of railway concessions leading to commercial monopoly. Frequent protests and warnings were addressed to Peking; and the Chinese were ready enough to give assurances representing wishes, which they were unable to carry out in the face of France's superior force. The only effective reply to the French claims then, it was held, was to be found in the grant of counter-concessions by China to England; and so the English secured a series of concessions and advances parallel to those granted to France, and in the same region. The agreements of 1886, 1890, 1893, 1894 and 1897 [23] opened trade and residence to British officials at Yatung, rectified the Burmese frontier, organized overland trade, opened the West River to seaborne trade, Wuchau being declared a treaty port. The most important result of English diplomacy was the passing of Burma, theretofore under Chinese suzerainty, under complete British rule through the so-called O'Connor Convention of July 24, 1886.[24] By Article II China agreed " that, in all matters whatever appertaining to the authority and rule which England is now exercising in Burma, England

[23] See Mayers, op. cit., pages 251 ff., and see also Rockhill, " Treaties and Conventions," Nos. 1 and 7.
[24] See " China," No. 5, 1886, C — 4861.

shall be free to do whatever she deems fit and proper."
In 1890 Sikkim followed the way of Burma.

But while the dependencies of China were dropping
from her in the south and southwest and while Korea
was preparing her independence, the conclusion of the
Chino-Japanese War marked the beginning of a series
of new events and the recognition of new political problems concerning China proper. The war disclosed the
utter military weakness of the Manchu Government,
and several great Powers were not slow in taking advantage of this fact by disintegrating Chinese territory
and pressing China for special and exclusive advantages.
The most important event at this time was the occupation
of the Liaotung peninsula and Port Arthur by Russia,
an occupation which had long been determined on and
which enabled Russia to obtain a stronger influence over
the Chinese at Peking. The occupation was preceded by
the seizure of Kiaochau by Germany, which had been
well aware of Russia's ambitions, and was immediately
followed by similar actions of Great Britain and
France.

By this territorial aggression the old method of negotiating by force was revived. But while the armed interference of Great Britain in former periods had secured
equal opportunities to all other nations, the actions of the
powers in the years 1897–1898 proved to be of an individual and selfish character. They disclosed the growth

of the new principle of preferential concessions, developing into the policy of " spheres of interest."   Before long
we find Germany maintaining that Shantung, as the
hinterland of Kiaochau, could not be open without reserve to the enterprise of others than Germans.   Almost
at the same moment, Russia was announcing that she
would not permit the Chinese provinces bordering on the
Russian frontiers to come under the influence of any
other nation.   She was pressing on to the economic as
well as the political control of north China.   While
France was aiming at the south, Japan claimed predominance in Fukien, and England in the Yangtsze-
Kiang region.

All these concessions were extorted from China practically without any compensation.   Stripped of her
power, China had to pay the penalty of an unsuccessful
war, and was forced to grant such privileges which she
had hitherto steadily refused.   The concessions were
either granted without excuse, or they were the penalties
of acts of violence on the part of the Chinese subjects,
the missionary being a favorite pretext.   But the penalty was usually out of all proportion to the crime, and
China had reason for regarding the policies adopted by
the European Powers as an open attack on the independence of the Empire.   And indeed the independence and
integrity of China seemed to have been severely menaced,
for it is evident that the vision of a " break up of China "

played a great rôle in the imagination of European statesmen.

At the same time the commercial and financial world was stirred with splendid visions of the long-deferred unconditional opening-up of China, and finance began to display interest in a country which presented unusual economic attractions. In this connection it is necessary to bear in mind the tremendous economic changes which had taken place in Europe towards the end of the nineteenth century. The immense development of the economic resources of Europe and the overproduction of capital resulted in an unprecedented outflow of capital to all parts of the world. The perfection of the joint stock company, and the general recognition granted to this form of organization, made it possible for capital successfully to undertake in distant lands enterprises which could not otherwise have been undertaken. The private speculator and especially the great financial interests appear in China and behind the latter is the whole diplomatic force of their respective countries; or the governments appear as the economic patrons of their subjects and promote or encourage financial enterprises in China. Finance takes the rôle which trade so successfully had played in its connection with foreign policy, the great and principal objects of finance being railway enterprises and political loans. Such were the economic forces behind the " battle of concessions."

CHAPTER II

THE aim of Britain, the greatest Asiatic power, was the maintenance of her economic preponderance. Since her interests existed in every port and her trade flourished in every province, she was bound to resent the attempt at closing any portion of China to her trade, and she had to oppose any measures which might tend to give undue advantage to another power. The policy of England, under the leadership of Lord Salisbury, was that known as the " open door " policy, its signification being that the door of trade should be kept open for Great Britain in every place where it was made available to any other country in China. To the demands for an " open door " were added the watchwords: " integrity of China " and " equal opportunity," all of which are constantly reappearing in the newspapers,[1] and in the official correspondence concerning the affairs of China.[2] But the British Government had to go beyond the mere proclamation of these principles, as long as other nations did not respect them. When Germany leased the territory of

---

[1] See, for instance, London *Times,* April 6, 1898, and otherwise.
[2] See " China," No. 1, 1899, Vol. CIX.

Kiaochau, Russia Port Arthur and Talienwan, and France Kuangchouwan, England was apparently unable to raise effective objections and resolved to follow the example of the others. The foreign office was especially worried about Russia's advance in the north, since Russia was considered England's great opponent in Asia. Lord Salisbury declared that " the balance of power in the Gulf of Pechili is materially altered by the surrender of Port Arthur by the Yamen to Russia." [3]   The English therefore entered into negotiations with the Yamen which resulted in the leasing of the harbor of Weihaiwei to England. A convention was signed on the first of July, 1898: " In order to provide Great Britain with a suitable naval harbor in North China and for the better protection of British commerce in the neighboring seas." [4] Of great significance for Great Britain's policy is the clause in the first paragraph in which China agrees to lease Weihaiwei " for so long a period as Port Arthur shall remain in the occupation of Russia."

In the meantime French plans had expanded with the success of their policy of pressure. France demanded the right to construct a railway from the Tongking frontier to Yunnan and a few other privileges, whereupon the British Government adopted the policy of counterconcessions. British policy and British demands are

[3] See " China," No. 1, 1898, Vol. CV, page 54.
[4] See " China," No. 1, 1899, Vol. CIX, page 199.

illustrated in the instructions of Mr. Balfour to Sir C. MacDonald of April 13, 1898:[5] " Inform Yamen that, although they have not followed our advice, we are anxious to maintain, as far as possible, integrity of China, and will, therefore, not make new territorial demands upon them. It is, however, absolutely necessary, if we are to pursue this policy, that they, on their side, should first immediately conclude negotiations — (a) for giving us all the land required for military defenses of Hongkong; (b) to fulfill their promise to make Nanking a Treaty port; (c) to give some railway concession; (d) an agreement as to the non-alienation of Kuangtung and Yunnan. In connection with condition (d), it is in the interests of the integrity of China and is justified by the proximity of Yunnan to Burma, and by our commercial preponderance in Kuangtung."

The first result of British demands was a convention for the extension of Hongkong, signed on June 9, 1898,[6] by which China granted a lease for ninety-nine years of 400 square miles of territory in the peninsula of Kowloon, immediately opposite to Hongkong. As to railway concessions mentioned by Mr. Balfour, England found herself soon in a position to press her demands, when the Peking-Hankow concession menaced England's interests in the Yangtsze Valley.

[5] See " China," No. 1, 1899, Vol. CIX, No. 21.
[6] See " China," No. 1, 1899, Vol. CIX, No. 174; see also Rockhill, op. cit., No. 12.

One of the first things undertaken by the British after the ratification of the Treaty of Tientsin, had been the exploitation of the Yangtsze-Kiang. Since British interests along the great valley were greater than those of other countries and as it was alike the most fertile, prosperous and densely populated region of China, it was essentially the most important British sphere of interest in that country. Hence the British Government, in order to prevent eventual inroads of other powers into this territory, exchanged in February, 1898, notes with the Chinese Government respecting the non-alienation of the Yangtsze-Region.[7] In this correspondence, which in its character is extremely vague, China gives an assurance that she would " never alienate any territory in the provinces adjoining the Yangtsze to any other power, whether under lease, mortgage, or any other designation." The conclusion of the agreement was highly welcomed by the British interests in China. Thus writes the China Association to Lord Salisbury: " The Association has ventured on former occasions to indicate the Yangtsze Valley as a region in which British interests must prevail. It welcomed with cordial satisfaction, therefore, the announcement that China had been led to promise that no portion of that area should be leased or ceded to a foreign power." [8]

[7] See "China," No. 2, 1898, Vol. CV; see also Rockhill, op. cit., No. 22.

[8] See "China," No. 1, 1899, Vol. CIX, No. 25.

British interests now were menaced, when, in 1897, a Belgian syndicate obtained a provisional concession for the great trunk line from Peking to Hankow.[9] There was clearly ground for Great Britain to be alarmed that Belgium served the plans of France and Russia. Lord Salisbury declared that "a concession of this nature is no longer a commercial or industrial enterprise and becomes a political movement against the British interests in the region of the Yangtsze. You should inform the Tsungli-Yamen that Her Majesty's Government cannot possibly continue to coöperate in a friendly manner in matters of interest to China, if, while preferential advantages are conceded to Russia in Manchuria and to Germany in Shantung these or other foreign Powers should also be offered special openings or privileges in the region of the Yangtsze. Satisfactory proposals will be forthcoming if the Chinese Government will invite the employment of British capital in the development of those provinces." [10]   Mr. MacDonald strongly protested, whereupon the Yamen assured the British minister that the Russians were not interested in the scheme, and that no agreement admitting the Russo-Chinese Bank to participation would ever receive the Imperial sanction.[11]   In spite of all protests the Chinese signed the final contract of the Peking Hankow Railway early in August, admit-

[9] See Rockhill, op. cit., No. 34.
[10] See "China," No. 1, 1899, Vol. CIX, No. 175.
[11] See "China," No. 1, 1899, Vol. CIX, Nos. 196, 263, 289.

ting the Russo-Chinese Bank to financial participation.[12]
The greatest objection which the British raised to the
contract was that the receipt and payment of funds by
the Russo-Chinese Bank, on behalf of the syndicate,
would pave the way to a future interference with the
construction and control of the line.   Mr. MacDonald
declared Russian admittance a " breach of faith " on the
side of the Chinese and demanded " reparation."   He
informed the Yamen that " Her Majesty's Government
considered that they had been badly treated by China in
the matter of railway concessions, and now demanded
from the Chinese Government the right for British
merchants to build the following lines upon the same
terms as those granted in the case of the Belgian line: —
Tientsin to Chinkiang (to be shared, if desired, with the
Germans and Americans), Honan and Shansi, Peking
syndicate lines to the Yangtsze; Kowloon to Canton;
Pukou to Sinyang; Soochow to Hangchow, with extension to Ningpo.   The lines from Shanghai to Nanking, and Shanhaikuan to Newchwang, I added, were
not included in this list, as preliminary agreements had
already been signed for them, and they might be considered settled." [13]   Mr. Balfour's instructions furthermore illustrate the great amount of pressure exacted by
Great Britain.   Mr. MacDonald was authorized to in-

[12] See " China," No. 1, 1899, Vol. CIX, Nos. 347 and 383.
[13] See " China," No. 1, 1899, Vol. CIX, No. 382.

form the Yamen that, " unless they agree at once, we shall regard their breach of faith concerning the Peking-Hankow Railway as an act of deliberate hostility against this country, and shall act accordingly. After consultation with the Admiral, you may give them the number of days or hours you think proper within which to send their reply." [14]

The Yamen, being aware of the concentration of the fleet, conceded everything.[15] Thus did Great Britain obtain her railway concessions. The total length of the lines conceded amounted to 2,800 miles extending over ten provinces, as compared to 1,530 Russian miles, the rest of the nations falling way below the Russian figure.[16] To England fell the lion's share of the " battle of concessions," as Lord Salisbury properly styled this " peaceful " conflict.[17]

But with that the " battle of concessions " was not finished. Russia considered Manchuria and Pechili her exclusive sphere of interest. She therefore pressed Peking for the removal of Mr. Kinder, an Englishman, from his position as superintendent of the Tientsin-Shanhaikuan Railway, demanding that the " line north of Shanhaikwan should be constructed by Russian engineers and with Russian capital." [18] Ignoring Russian de-

[14] See " China," No. 1, 1899, Vol. CIX, No. 286.
[15] See " China," No. 1, 1899, Vol. CIX, No. 324.
[16] Detailed analysis will be given below.
[17] See " China," No. 1, 1899, Vol. CIX, No. 232.
[18] See " China," No. 2, 1899, Vol. CIX, No. 2.

mands, the Hongkong and Shanghai Bank entered into an agreement to furnish the capital to construct a railway between Peking and Newchwang, taking a mortgage on the line.[19]   This caused much irritation in Russia and the relations between Russia and England became more strained than they were before.   The friction which had arisen over railways rendered it desirable to come to an understanding in regard to mutual privileges and spheres of interest in China.   After a long series of negotiations an exchange of notes was effected between the two countries in April, 1899.[20]   The text of the agreement is as follows: " 1. Great Britain engages not to seek for her own account, or on behalf of British subjects or of others, any railway concessions to the north of the Great Wall of China, and not to obstruct, directly or indirectly, applications for railway concessions in that region supported by the Russian Government. 2. Russia, on her part, engages not to seek for her own account, or on behalf of Russian subjects or of others, any railway concessions in the basin of the Yangtsze, and not to obstruct, directly or indirectly, applications for railway concessions in that region supported by the British Government." By a supplementary note, the rights of the British and Chinese Corporation, under the loan contract, over the section from Shan-

[19] See " China," No. 2, 1899, Vol. CIX, Nos. 4 and 10.
[20] See " China," No. 2, 1899, Vol. CIX, No. 129.

haikuan to Newchwang were reserved, "and the Chinese Government may appoint both an English engineer and a European accountant to supervise the construction of the line in question, and the expenditure of the money appropriated to it. But it remains understood that this fact cannot be taken as constituting a right of property or foreign control, and that the line in question is to remain a Chinese line, under the control of the Chinese Government, and cannot be mortgaged or alienated to a non-Chinese company!" With this agreement the "sphere of interest" theory was considerably strengthened.

In the case of the other trunk line from the north, that from Tientsin to Chinkiang on the Yangtsze, England inevitably came into collision with the interests of Germany. The English were bidding for construction or at least participation in construction of this line. The German minister, in 1898, was objecting that no line could be constructed through Shantung without the concurrence of Germany. In August, 1898, Baron Heyking informed the British minister of his instruction from his home government, of which the respective passage reads as follows: "Should the Chinese Government decide to grant a concession for the Tientsin-Chinkiang Railway regardless of German claims, you are instructed to oppose such a decision, and, should it be necessary, you may inform the Chinese Government that the German Government would consider as ' non avenu ' any concession in that province, and would reserve the right of making the Chinese Government responsible for any such concession in the event of its being granted by them." [21]   It has to be remarked here, that England as early as April, 1898, had formally declared to Germany: " that in establishing herself at Weihaiwei she has no intention of injuring or contesting the rights and interests of Germany in the Province of Shantung, or of creating difficulties for her in that province.   It is especially understood that England will not construct any railroad communication from Weihaiwei and the district leased therewith into the interior of the Province of Shantung." [22] But a mutual official declaration as to the respective spheres of interest had not taken place.   Both governments considered that a specific delimitation would " not be opportune, and that a friendly understanding in each case as it arose would be preferable." [23]   Such friendly compromise was finally concluded between the respective German and British financial interests, on Sept. 1st and 2nd, 1898, at London.   The text reads, in parts, as follows : [24]

   1. British sphere of interest, viz. :

   " The Yangtsze Valley subject to the connection of the

[21] See " China," No. 1, 1899, Vol. CIX, No. 305.
[22] See " China," No. 1, 1899, Vol. CIX, No. 31.
[23] See " China," No. 1, 1899, Vol. CIX, No. 307.
[24] See " China," No. 1, 1899, Vol. CIX, No. 312.

Shantung lines to the Yangtsze at Chinkiang; the provinces south of the Yangtsze; the Province of Shansi with connection to the Peking-Hankow line at a point south of Chengting and a connecting line to the Yangtsze Valley, crossing the Hoangho Valley."

2. German sphere of interest, viz.:

" The Province of Shantung and the Hoangho Valley with connection to Tientsin and Chengting, or other point of the Peking-Hankow line, in the south with connection to the Yangtsze at Chinkiang or Nanking. The Hoangho Valley is understood to be subject to the connecting lines in Shansi forming part of the British sphere of interest, and to the connecting line to the Yangtsze Valley, also belonging to the said sphere of interest."

This was agreed to with the modification that the line from Tientsin to Chinkiang be financed jointly, constructed separately according to the respective spheres through which the lines were to run, and, on completion, to be worked for joint account.

The various railway questions had led to many critical moments for Great Britain in 1898. In order to protect her own interests, she was forced to desist somewhat from the traditional open door policy. Standing alone she had to fear that she might not be able to sustain China's absolute integrity against the aggression of other powers. A union of aim between her and any other nation or a combination of nations she recognized would go far to end the rivalries which threatened to partition China. Consequently, she eagerly seized the opportunity of expressing her adherence to the open door policy in replying favorably to Mr. Hay's propositions of 1899.[25]   The United States, though it has never taken an active part in the opening up of China, had gradually developed a very considerable interest in the country, which it was eager to see preserved. In this year the United States sent a circular letter to the European Powers to seek information as to the possibility of coming to an understanding in regard to the maintenance of treaty rights, and the safeguarding of the integrity of the Empire. The requirements of the policy of equal opportunity known as the " open door " were categorically set out in this circular,[26] with the object of obtaining the definite adherence of the various powers to its support. The replies of all the powers concerned was in the affirmative. England's attitude is expressed by Lord Salisbury in his acknowledgment of the last of the communications from the American minister: " I may assure Your Excellency that the policy consistently advocated by this country is one of securing equal opportunity for the subjects and citizens of all nations in regard to commercial enterprise in China, and from this policy her Majesty's Government has no intention or desire to de-

[25] See Rockhill, op. cit., No. 28, and Malloy, op. cit., I, 244 ff.
[26] See Chapter VII.

part." [27]   A similar policy was contained in an agreement identical in its contents to the note of Mr. Hay, concluded between Great Britain and Germany in October, 1900.[28]

The unfortunate Chinese officials in the meantime had learned that in spite of all the assurances of the foreigners, friendly intercourse might be as dangerous as open hostility. They took the lessons of the extorted concessions to heart and attempted to apply their experience in dealing with the railway problem. Fearing that railways constructed by foreign capital might later be made an excuse for territorial claims, they put every possible obstacle in the way of such undertakings. Thus they steadily refused the promised British concessions in Yunnan and decided towards the end of 1898 not to give any new railway concessions exclusively to foreigners. To that end they issued regulations on November 19, 1898, for mines and railways in China, which throw light on the real motives of Chinese policy.[29] In these it was stated that the concessions in Manchuria, Shantung and Luzchan (referring to the Russian, German and French spheres) " are affected by international relations, and therefore will not be allowed to form precedents either for Chinese or foreigners." In Article 9 it is required that Chinese capital was to be employed as far as

[27] See Rockhill, op. cit., page 191.
[28] See Rockhill, op. cit., No. 14.
[29] See Rockhill, op. cit., No. 48.

possible, and that in all cases of concessions an endeavor must be made to have the Chinese part of the capital in such enterprises the greater proportion, at least a minimum of three-tenths of the total. By another rule, as an inducement to the natives, rewards were to be granted to Chinese promoters raising a capital of 500,000 taels, or contriving that half the shares in a company were Chinese-owned. The essence of the whole matter was summed up in the thirteenth clause: " In order to protect the sovereign rights of China, the control of all railways and mining companies, irrespective of the foreign capital concerned, must remain in the hands of the Chinese merchants." The regulations clearly meant nothing else than an absolute bar to the further investment of foreign capital. China once more tried to rid herself from the grip of foreign influence. But she found herself unable to do so.

While they were not at all without success as far as concessions are concerned they became, on the other hand, more and more dependent upon the foreigners in another phase of finance. The financial necessities of China, a result of the Japanese War, and the indemnity had provided another means of dependence on the foreigners and a new lever for inducing the acceptance of western demands. The different loans contracted in this connection amounted to L54,455,000 and were divided into one Franco-Russian Government loan and

two joint Anglo-German Government loans of 1896 and
1898, each being L16,000,000.[30]　The maritime customs
served as security under the Inspector-General of Maritime Customs.　A special assurance to Great Britain was
that the Inspector should be an Englishman so long as
England should maintain her preponderance of trade.[31]
This was necessary since Russia was trying to insist on
a Russian for the post, which until then had so successfully been administered by Sir Robert Hart.

The permanent foreign pressure for concessions, the
territorial acquisitions and the constant attempts at intro-
ducing western ideas into China, or in other words, the
period of 1897–1898, had brought about a strong anti-
foreign sentiment all over China.　The result was the
Boxer Rebellion of 1900.　Referring to its causes,
Lancelot Lawton quotes from one of the proclamations
issued by the rebel leader Yu Tung Chen, who wrote:[32]
" These foreigners, under pretext of trading and teaching Christianity, are in reality taking away the land,
food, and clothing of the people; besides overturning the
teaching of the sages, they are poisoning us with opium
and ruining us with debauchery.　Since the time of Tao
Kuang, they seized our territory and cheated us out of
our money; they have eaten our children as food and

[30] See " China Year Book," 1914; see Chapter VIII.
[31] See " China," No. 1, 1899, Vol. CIX, No. 20.
[32] Lancelot Lawton, " The Empires of the Far East," Vol. I, page
2.

piled up the public debt as high as the hills; they have burnt our palaces and overthrown our tributary states, occupied Shanghai, devastated Formosa, forcibly opened Kiaochau, and now wish to divide up China like a melon." This passage shows that the Boxer rising though primarily fanatical in its aspect, was none the less evidence of the awakening of a national spirit. But once more the Chinese were forced to recognize the superiority of foreign arms and foreign methods. The rebellion resulted in humiliation for China.

In connection with the Boxer event and its sequels there are two points of supreme interest. The first is the resulting political constellation. The campaign disclosed Russia's diplomatic duplicity. Her policy was to back up the Chinese against the European Powers in order that she might pose as the protector of China for her own ends. She displayed a friendship for China and a protective attitude directed against foreign, especially English, aggression.[33]

England was well aware of the menace which Russia's policy meant to her. She saw in Russia her traditional enemy more than ever. She strongly resented the forward policy of Russia in China, but found herself unable to check it single handed. Consequently she looked for an alliance which might restore the equilibrium of power in the Far East. The ally she found in Japan. The

[33] See Chapter III.

island kingdom considered itself equally menaced by Russia's aggression, which already extended to the southern shore of Manchuria and which began to make itself felt in Korea, the independence of which kingdom was of vital interest to Japan. In seeking among the powers one who would support and finance her in active opposition to Russia's, Japan's inclinations leaned towards Great Britain, who formerly had refused to join other powers in turning her out of Port Arthur. Great Britain, on the other hand, was almost forced to throw in her lot with Japan, since Japan otherwise had to come to an understanding with Russia which would have destroyed the British position in China almost entirely. The Anglo-Japanese Offensive and Defensive Alliance concluded on January 30, 1902, then, was intended to check the encroachments of Russia upon Northern China and adjacent territories and to safeguard British and Japanese commercial and financial interests in those regions; [34] or as the treaty expresses it: the two governments are " specially interested in maintaining the independence and territorial integrity of the Empire of China and the Empire of Korea, and in securing equal opportunities in those countries for the commerce and industry of all nations." Its significance is, according to Aubert, the addition of a maritime sphere of influence policy to the already existing territorial sphere of influence policy,

[34] See Rockhill, op. cit., No. 16.

— the English sphere being the Indian Ocean and the Japanese sphere the seas of the Far East.[35]

The second point of importance in reference to the Boxer rising, is the indemnity imposed upon China according to Article VI of the Final Protocol signed on completion of negotiations by the various Powers at Peking on September 7, 1901.[36] The indemnity amounted to L67,500,000, Great Britain's share being L7,425,000.[37] It proved to be a tremendous burden upon China's budget. China certainly had to pay heavily for the Boxer rising, which, after all, was nothing else than a protest against the aggression of 1898.

In Article XI of the Peking Protocol the Chinese Government had also agreed to negotiate the amendments to the existing treaties of commerce and navigation deemed necessary by the foreign governments. Accordingly Great Britain concluded on September 5, 1902, a new commercial treaty with China, the so-called Mackay Treaty, which provided for further trade facilities and opened a few new treaty ports.[38]

[35] L. Aubert, " Paix Japonaise," page 50: " A la politique des sphères d'influence territoriales en Chine, le traité anglo-japonais substitue une politique de sphères d'influence maritimes. D'Aden jusqu'au détroit de la Pérouse, Anglais et Japonais se partagent la maîtrise de la mer. Les mers extrême-orientales sont laissées à l'influence spéciale du Japon, tandis que l'Angleterre fortifie sa position dans l'océan Indien ; chacun son domaine."
[36] See Rockhill, op. cit., No. 15.
[37] See Chapter VIII.
[38] See Rockhill, op. cit., No. 18.

After the successful conclusion of the alliance with
Japan, and the treaty with China, England could, at least
for the time being, breathe freer.   Having cleared the
horizon of menacing clouds, the government left the long
deferred and hoped for expansion of trade and the development of the railroad schemes to the parties directly
interested.   Excepting official support given to the Hongkong and Shanghai Banking Corporation and its allied
interests, the British Government retired from its labors,
so to speak, and from now on did little in protecting or
promoting national or individual interests.   " Therefore
when questions arose from the evasion or repudiation of
China's obligations in the matter of railways and mining
enterprises, not to speak of everyday commercial cases,
the nature of the support rendered by His Majesty's Government took the form of permitting the parties concerned to make the best compromise possible and pro-
claiming the results (when there were any) as triumphs
of British diplomacy." [39]

It is of importance to know that British policy at this
period, as on former occasions, continued to be influenced
primarily by the English business world in China.   The
Chinese trade had gradually built up predominant local
interests in the hands of a few powerful firms.   While
British foreign policy usually is largely directed by public opinion, the constant absence of any public opinion

[39] Bland, op. cit., page 273.

regarding China, based on a lack of interest in this remote country, had caused the policy of the Foreign Office to be guided by the advice of the individuals and firms most prominently associated with China. It was assumed that those who had long experience and represented special interests should frequently be consulted by the Foreign Office. The "China Association," for instance, has for many years rendered notable services to the advancement of Great Britain's interests in the Far East. It was this body that attracted Lord Salisbury's attention to the dangerous activities of France in southern China and Russia in Manchuria.[40]

As the problems of China became more and more involved and complicated, and as railway construction and finance began, the activities of the vested interests naturally widened and added the cares of finance to the former protection of trade. "As a direct result of the situation," writes the *Far Eastern Review,* "arising from the keen struggle for railway concessions in 1898 to strengthen the political hold of the European powers on China, the organization of a purely British company became essential to act as the official instrument for the execution of the concessions extracted from the Chinese Government."[41] The forming of such company fell naturally to the Hongkong and Shanghai Banking Cor-

[40] "China," No. 1, 1899, Vol. CIX, No. 25.
[41] "Far Eastern Review," Vol. 10, page 297.

poration. This bank was the predominant British financial institution, and its power can hardly be exaggerated, since the entire British community in China depended more or less on its credit facilities.

The bank, having on its Board of Directors the principal partners of the great German trading firms, had up to this time been operating under an agreement with the official German Banking Syndicate for mutual participation in administrative and railway loans to China.[42] When the battle of concessions began and the " sphere of interest " policy became generally recognized, the Hong-kong and Shanghai Banking Corporation, foreseeing the great advantages and profits to be derived as the representative British organization for the railway development of British policy, terminated their working arrangement with the strong German syndicate, and the manager on April 4th, 1898, directed a note to the Foreign Office to the following effect:

" I have the honor to acquaint you that the arrangements under which this bank has hitherto worked with the German Syndicate for the construction of railways in China has been terminated by mutual consent, It is now agreed that the German Syndicate and ourselves shall each work separately.

" I may here mention that the German Syndicate, always

[42] See Kent, " Railway Enterprise in China," page 150. See also Chapter VIII.

a powerful combination, has of late consolidated its position very much, and now includes all houses of any importance in Germany. It also enjoys the confidence of, and receives the support of, the German Government.

" In order that British commercial interests may be fully represented, and that we shall be in a better position to cope with the powerful combination now opposed to us in China, the bank has decided to form a strong representative and influential Syndicate to deal with railway construction in China. . . .

" In the meantime, I trust the explanation I have given will warrant you in giving the necessary instructions to Sir Claude MacDonald to give Messrs. Jardine, Matheson and Co., and the bank such support as they may require." [43]

The result of this letter was the early organization of the British and Chinese Corporation, Ltd., formed by the Hongkong and Shanghai Banking Corporation and the firm of Jardine, Matheson and Co. This strong, representative and influential syndicate has been able since to command, with the exception of the Peking Syndicate — whose activities however lay in another direction — a monopoly of the British Government's support. This corporation contracted henceforth with the Chinese Government the construction of all the great British built

[43] See " China," No. 1, 1899, Vol. CIX, No. 5.

railroads in China. "From time to time," says the *Far Eastern Review,* "other British railway constructors endeavored to secure a footing in China, but were compelled to retire after severe financial losses and leave the field to the undisputed control of the official commercial organization." [44] Exclusive official support was still enjoyed during the international loan negotiations, when the British Government repeatedly assured the syndicate of its protection.[45] And it was mainly owing to the failure of these negotiations that the field for financial enterprise was finally opened to other British concerns.

The monopoly exercised by the syndicate within the British sphere and under Government support was a monopoly of rights to contract railway construction at the exclusion of non-British as well as other British interests. On the strength of this monopoly the syndicate concluded agreements with the Chinese Government, by which it was granted a certain amount of "control" to be exercised within the sphere. "Control" indeed was uppermost in the minds of the syndicate as well as of the British Government. The fact that "foreign control" was assured in the Peking-Hankow agreement, that foreign political influence might menace British preponderance in the Yangtsze Valley, and that "by differential rates and privileges the managers of the railways

[44] See "Far Eastern Review," Vol. X, page 298.
[45] See "China," No. 2, 1912, Vol. CXXI, No. 1 to 7; see also Chapter VIII.

may strangle our trade " worried British officials considerably.[46]   Terms and privileges equal to those accorded to other nations were vehemently demanded. But we have to emphasize that the British Government, though it had forced the Chinese Government to grant railway concessions to British subjects within the sphere, had no part whatsoever in construction or control and it was not even a party to the signing or wording of the railway agreements or other contracts — with the exception of railways and also loans to be under international control.[47]

To determine the amount and degree of control exercised by the British syndicate we now have to turn to the respective clauses of the railway agreements.   The first railway contracted was the section Shanhaikuan-Newchwang of the Imperial Railways of North China. The preliminary agreement was signed on June 7, 1898, and the final railway loan agreement on Oct. 10, 1898, between the syndicate and the Administrator General of the Railways of North China, acting under authority of the Imperial Chinese Government.[48]   The principal clauses, establishing control, read as follows:

In Article 1:   The Corporation agrees to issue on behalf of the Administrator-General a sterling loan for the

[46] See " China," No. 1, 1899, Vol. CIX, Nos. 135 and 232.
[47] See Chapter VIII.
[48] See Rockhill, op. cit., Nos. 42 and 46.

amount of L2,300,000. (The term of the loan being 45 years: Art. 9.)

In Article 3: This loan shall be a first charge upon the security of the permanent way, rolling stock, and entire property, with the freight and earnings of the existing lines between Peking and Shanhaikuan, and on the freights and earnings of the new lines when constructed.

In Article 4: The principal and interest of this loan are guaranteed by the Imperial Government of China, and in the event of default in payment of interest or repayment of principal at due date, the Corporation shall immediately notify the Imperial Government of China thereof, and the Imperial Government of China will thereupon provide the funds necessary to meet such payment in sterling in London. In the event of the Imperial Government of China being unable to provide the funds necessary to meet a payment of interest or principal, when called upon by the Corporation to do so in terms of this clause, the said railway lines and the entire property shall thereupon be handed over to the representatives deputed by the Corporation to manage, on their behalf, until principal and interest of the loan have been redeemed in full, when the management will revert to the Railway Administration. . . .

This arrangement, which differs from other contracts in that the Administrator-General retains control of the railway lines so long as the principal and interest of this loan are regularly paid, has been agreed to in consequence of the friendly relations which have long existed between the Contracting Parties.

In Article 6: During the currency of this loan the Chief Engineer of railway shall be a British subject. The principal members of the railway staff shall be capable and experienced Europeans, who shall be, as at present, appointed by the Administrator-General of the Railways. . . .

In addition to the above, a capable and efficient European Railway Accountant shall be appointed, with full powers to organize and direct the keeping of the railway accounts, and to act with the Administrator-General and the Chief Engineer of the railway in the supervision of receipts and expenditure.

In Article 8: All receipts and earnings of the lines herein specified shall be paid into the credit of the Railway Administration with the Hongkong and Shanghai Banking Corporation, Tientsin. . . .

In reimbursement of expenses incurred in connection with the distribution of the service to the bondholders of the principal and interest of the loan, the Hongkong and Shanghai Banking Corporation, Tientsin, shall receive from the Railway Administration a commission of $\frac{1}{4}$ per cent. on the annual loan service, which will be included in the yearly Schedule for the same.

In Article 14: All bonds and coupons and payments

made and received in connection with this loan shall be exempt from Chinese taxes and imposts forever.

The next railway of importance contracted was the line from Shanghai to Nanking. The preliminary agreement was signed on May 13, 1898, and the final agreement on July 9, 1903, both between the syndicate and the Director General of the Chinese Imperial Railway acting under authority of the Imperial Chinese Government. The final agreement provided in particular for the following terms: [49] The corporation agrees to issue a loan not exceeding L3,250,000, for which Chinese Government Bonds are to be issued. The duration is fifty years. The Chinese Railway administration undertakes to buy and pay for the land required. The loan shall be secured by mortgage on all lands, material, rolling stock, buildings and property and no further mortgage or loan shall be created on the said lines. In order to provide for a final authority, a " Board of Control " is created to be composed of the Director General of the Chinese Railway Administration and nominee of his, together with three representatives of the syndicate. The Chief Engineer, at the same time Chief Administrator, shall be nominated by the syndicate with the concurrence of the Director General, and shall be paid by the Chinese railway administration. The residue of the net profits in each year after paying the sum annually due for inter-

[49] See Rockhill, op. cit., No. 39.

est and redemption of the loan and all other sums which may be due to the syndicate, shall be divided into five shares, one to be retained by the syndicate as remuneration for superintendence and services; the syndicate shall receive five per cent. on the entire cost of all materials purchased for the railway. Finally it is to be mentioned that all bonds are exempted from taxation. The money actually lent was L2,250,000 in 1904 and L630,000 in 1907.[50]

The Canton-Kowloon Railway agreement between the Board of Foreign Affairs of the Chinese Government and the British and Chinese Corporation, Ltd., concluded on the 7th of March, 1907, contains control provisions similar to those of the two preceding agreements.[51]   Imperial Chinese Government bonds are to be issued for the amount of L1,500,000 similar to the bonds of the Shanghai-Nanking Railway, with the railway as first mortgage security therefor.   The loan is to be secured by a specific and legal first mortgage in favor of the Corporation upon all lands, materials, rolling stock, buildings, property and premises, of every description purchased or to be purchased for the railway, and on the railway itself, as and when constructed, and on the revenue of all descriptions derivable therefrom.   A British Engineer-in-Chief and a British Chief accountant are to be associated with

[50] See "China Year Book," 1913, Chapter XVI.
[51] See Kent, op. cit., Appendix F, No. 4.

the Chinese Managing Director.   It is also agreed, that if
interest or principal in accordance with the amortization
schedule is not paid on due date, the whole railway with
all its appurtenances mortgaged to the Corporation for
the bondholders, shall be handed over to the Corporation.
The Corporation are appointed trustees for the bondholders.   In remuneration for all services rendered by
the Corporation, during construction, the Corporation
shall receive the sum of L35,000.   The handling of all
funds is entrusted to the Hongkong and Shanghai Banking Corporation.

Next in importance to the agreements concluded by the
British and Chinese Corporation come those concluded
by the Peking Syndicate, a powerful Anglo-Italian corporation.[52]   Although the driving power of the syndicate was an Italian subject, Mr. Luzatti, the British Foreign Office used a considerable amount of " pressure "
upon the Chinese Government towards obtaining the
grant of the concessions in question.[53]   By the agreement from May 21, 1898, the syndicate obtained the
sole right to open and work the coal and iron deposits
of central and southern Shansi and Honan and the petroleum deposits of the entire province, and secured the
right to construct and operate all necessary railways to
maintain trunk lines or navigable waters for exporting

[52] See Kent, op. cit., Chapter XIII.
[53] See " China," No. 1, 1899, Vol. CIX, No. 6, 106, and otherwise.

the mining products.[54] " All matters of administration, exploitation, employees, and finances shall be controlled by the Board of Directors of the Peking Syndicate, and the Chief of the Shansi Bureau of trade shall coöperate. . . . Each line must have one foreign and one Chinese manager, the foreigner to control the works, the Chinese to attend to all matters between natives and foreigners. Accounts will be kept by the foreign system."   By the agreement for the Construction of a Railway from Taokow to Chinghua by the syndicate, the Chinese Government agreed that the railway for all practical purposes was to remain under the control of the syndicate until the bonds have been secured.[55]   The amount of the loan was L700,000 and was secured by a first mortgage on the railway, its line, rolling stock and earnings.   A commission of one-fourth of one per cent. on the amount of interest coupons paid, and the like commission on all bonds drawn for payment was to be paid to the syndicate. Finally, according to the additional working agreement was the syndicate entitled to receive from the Imperial Chinese Railway Administration 20 per cent. of the surplus of each year.

Although these control provisions appear to be very favorable to the syndicate, they remain nevertheless insignificant, since this railway is very short and of abso-

[54] See Rockhill, op. cit., No. 40.
[55] See Kent, op. cit., Appendix C, Nos. 1 and 2.

lutely secondary importance when compared with the valuable mining concessions. The " control " provisions are in substance similar to those of the British and Chinese Corporations' agreements. In order to reduce the above enumerated control provisions to their essence and true meaning we can not do any better than use the words of Mr. Willard Straight and Mr. Kent. Mr. Straight writes in " China's Loan Negotiations " : [56]

" Control in the at present accepted sense of the word was first embodied in the agreement made by the Chinese Government in 1898, with the British and Chinese Corporation, for a loan to the Imperial Railways of North China.

" Under this agreement, and in several others concluded at about this time, the lenders, besides securing a first mortgage on the railway whose construction they financed, were entitled to a share in the profits of the line.

" For this reason and also because of the inexperience of the Chinese in railway matters, the bankers required assurances that the loaned funds should be so expended that the mortgaged property would constitute a sufficient security.

" They furthermore obtained a certain share in the management of these lines in order that there should be secured therefrom an adequate return (to a certain percentage of which the banks were entitled), and to prevent

[56] See Straight, op. cit., page 131.

the administrative inefficiency and fraud which they feared if the operation of these railways were placed entirely in Chinese hands."

Mr. Kent's summary of the aspects of the contracts is similar: [57]

" Firstly, the syndicate is given the right to construct the line, and in return for its trouble in this connection it is in most cases allowed a sum equivalent to 5 per cent. on the total cost.   It is this right which presumably gives rise to the idea of concession.

" Secondly, on completion of the line it is placed in some cases under a theoretically joint Chinese and foreign control, in which in practice the foreign element predominates.   In other cases the Chinese have merely a consultative voice.

" Thirdly and lastly, at this stage, or rather from the time of the issue of the loan, the syndicate become trustees for the bondholders, and it is easy to see that, in the nature of things, the loan being secured by a first mortgage upon the railway, the position of the syndicate for all practical purposes must be that of mortgagees in possession."

Such are the underlying principles of the agreements which confer these rights, which for want of a more precise term we call, and shall continue to call, concessions.   The details, of course, vary.

[57] See Kent, op. cit., page 95.

According to Mr. Kent the agreements are in the nature of underwriting contracts, and the indirect profits to the syndicate accruing therefrom are very handsome.[58] " The contracting syndicate undertakes to provide 90 per cent., for example, of a loan of so many millions of pounds or dollars, as the case may be, repayable at a certain specified time and bearing interest at the rate of 5 per cent. per annum; it takes its chance of being able to float the loan upon the public at a higher percentage of its nominal value. What has happened in most cases is that on every L100 bond, for example, issued by the Chinese Government the latter received L90, while the syndicate have succeeded in getting them taken up at L97 or thereabouts, thus securing a respectable margin on the transaction."

Another source of profit to the banks as well as to English industries, was the provisions which made the syndicate the purchasing agents of materials and rolling stock. Outside of the fact that the corporation was to receive on the average 5 per cent. commission of the entire cost of all materials purchased, the materials were naturally almost exclusively purchased in England.[59] Although all materials were nominally to be purchased in the open market, the usual clause that " at equal rates and qualities, goods of British manufacture shall be given

[58] See Kent, op. cit., page 94.
[59] See also Chapter VIII.

preference over other goods of foreign origin " provided
an opportunity for almost exclusive purchase in England.
Thus writes the *Far Eastern Review,* referring to the
open market provision: " We find, however, that, notwithstanding the specific agreement the purchases were
made exclusively in London without reference to the
lowest price or open tenders." [60]

On the strength of the foregoing analysis we now draw
the conclusion that British control in China consists of
nothing more than safeguards for the protection of
the bondholders and bankers, guaranteeing proper loan
fund expenditure and adequate return.   British control
in China, exercised exclusively by private corporations, is
therefore essentially financial and non-political.

Its non-political character may be further illustrated
by the fact that the syndicate, in spite of its monopolistic
rights, admitted non-British interests to participation in
its privileges within the British sphere.

On February 1, 1899, the British and Chinese Corporation and the American China Development Company,
the latter having no exclusive government support, made
an agreement that each party should offer to the other a
participation of one-half of its own interest in any business hereafter obtained by it in China, excluding, however, a number of agreements which had been entered

[60] See " Far Eastern Review," Vol. VIII, page 82. See also
Straight, op. cit., page 123.

into previously by either party.[61]   This agreement, however, was terminated later.

In 1905 the British and Chinese Corporation, the Peking Syndicate and French bankers joined for general participation as to railway construction in the Yangtsze Valley, and especially in the regions north of the Yangtsze Valley,[62] namely, for the construction of the Pukow-Sinyang and Sinyang-Chengtu or Hankow-Chengtu railways.

One of the objectives of the British and Chinese Corporation had been a railway from Pukow to Sinyang and its eventual extension to Chengtu.   The Peking Syndicate, however, had planned a line which would seriously compete with the British and Chinese Corporations' line. " This and other considerations led to an amalgamation of the two companies for all future railroad development north of the Yangtsze," says Kent.[63]   The combination was henceforth known as the Chinese Central Railways, Ltd.   At the same time a group of French and Belgian capitalists, headed by the Banque de l'Indo-Chine, were also interested in securing the concession for a line from the Hankow-Sinyang district westwards to Chengtu.[64] To avoid competition the British combination entered

[61] See Rockhill, op. cit., No. 49.
[62] See Laboulaye, " Les Chemins de fer en Chine," pages 182 and 206.
[63] See Kent, op. cit., page 128.
[64] See " Far Eastern Review," Vol. X, page 298.

into negotiations with the French capitalists for joint
construction of the lines in question, absorbing their
interests into the Chinese Central Railways, Ltd. The
Pukow-Sinyang line was, however, eventually constructed
as a purely British line.[65]

As early as 1895 the Hongkong and Shanghai Banking Corporation had entered into an agreement with
the Deutsch Asiatische Bank to share all Chinese Government business thereafter obtained by either party. The
resulting financial transactions, done in common, and
especially the Tientsin-Pukow agreement with its important control provisions, shall be analyzed in the Chapter on
" International Action." Their agreement as to mutual
participation was terminated in 1898, with the exception
of the Tientsin-Chinkiang-Pukow Railway, and the bankers agreed to respect their mutual spheres.[66] As a consequence the Germans abstained for several years from
demanding participation in the railway enterprises within
the Yangtsze sphere. But, presumably owing to the
political and economic changes after the conclusion of the
Russo-Japanese War, and owing to the increasing competition for a share in the benefits of Young China's
promised development of trade and industries, the German bank around 1908 changed its policy. It henceforth
demanded rights of participation under the terms of the
former agreement and intended to compete for railway

[65] See below, page 76.   [66] See above, page 46.

and other Chinese Government loans, in the Yangtsze Valley and elsewhere, unless admitted on terms of equality. The British financiers acquiesced in the German demand for participation, and the Germans associated with the British and French interests in the syndicate known as the Chinese Central Railways, Ltd. The activities of this " Tripartite " and, after the admission of the United States, the " Four Nations " group from now on are cosmopolitan in character and consequently shall be dealt with in detail in the Chapter on " International Action."

The admission of German participation with the Anglo-French Combination in the Yangtsze railway loans and in an area which had been recognized as reserved for the British, was an event sufficiently important to provoke criticism, such for instance as has been forthcoming from Mr. J. O. P. Bland in his excellent book on " Recent Events and Present Policies in China." [67] His criticism may be summarized as follows: That British and French financiers worked in common is easily explained by the excellent relation then and thereafter existing between the two countries; but that German and British financial interests should continue to coöperate in the Far East, while there was friction between the two countries at home, was a matter of much surprise to the English world, and the British bank having for years

[67] See Bland, op. cit., pages 273 ff.

enjoyed a monopoly of British Government support and become identified with British enterprise of far-reaching political importance, could not openly endorse the German claims without arousing opposition in England. The correspondent of *The Times* at Peking, expressed the general wonder that " the British Government should delegate to one British bank, which is naturally compelled to consider financial rather than national interests, the right to assist the extension of German influence." [68] It was demanded that the Government should organize and direct the use of British capital as a weapon of offense and defense and that it should follow the example of other countries and notably that of Germany where the financiers are obliged to conform strictly to the political directions of their Governments who are profiting by the laisser-aller methods of Great Britain.

The reasons that the Foreign Office showed no appreciation of the fact that other nations were successfully developing their rights of railway construction to the supposed detriment of Great Britain, and that no strong national policy could be expected, is on the one hand evidence of the absence of an effective force of public opinion.   For with the exception of very rare cases England's policy follows and does not lead public opinion. This is illustrated in a manifesto issued by the China League in February, 1901, wherein the following passage

[68] London. *Times,* May 9, 1909.

occurs: " At a time when the future of China hangs
in the balance, when the maintenance of our position
and trade in that Empire (that is to say, the welfare of
Great Britain in years to come) depends on the immediate policy of her majesty's Government and the action
of the British representative in the Concert of the Powers
at Peking: at such a time, the Imperial Parliament, its
attention apparently concentrated on personal explana-
tions of unimportant matters, enunciates no policy on
the Far Eastern question. Statesmen on both sides of
the House, and publicists of all shades of opinion, remain
silent in regard to the crises, offering no solution calculated to protect British interests. A debate on the
China question attracts less attention than a minor question of parochial Government." [69]

Furthermore, considering the situation as a whole and
having reference to the particular history of British-
Chinese relations and the various experiences of the Government, we are faced with the fact that the Government
finally was wearied by the futilities of the many negotiations and the ever increasing complexities of the situation. Great Britain's foreign policy in China, consistent with the traditions of British statesmanship, continued to be guided by the old traditional " laisser-faire "
and free trade principles, which had made the Empire
great. Therefore it left the control of Britain's financial

[69] See Bland, op. cit., page 270.

interests to the parties directly interested. And there is little wonder that the business of the British Syndicate, being unhampered by governmental interference or restriction, speedily assumed cosmopolitan character. For in its cosmopolitan tendencies, which are towards elimination of competition and towards consolidation, British finance is quite in harmony with leading British economic thought.

According to Mr. Hobson and other prominent economists the conception of nations as hostile competitors in world finance is economically unsound.[70] International finance is peace-loving, since the coöperation of the financiers of the various countries in business enterprises in all parts of the world is binding up the prosperity of each individual country intimately with the welfare of all other countries. Says Hobson: "Modern finance is the great sympathetic system in an economic organism in which political divisions are of constantly diminishing importance." [71]

That the policy of non-interference — barren of deep laid plans such as characterize the policies of other Powers in China, and at times criticized as suicidal to British prestige and British economic interests — has by no means handicapped the tremendous growth of British

[70] See J. A. Hobson, "Work and Wealth," Chapter XVII; see also Same, "An Economic Interpretation of Investment," passim, and J. H. Withers, "International Finance," pages 93 ff.

[71] See Hobson, "Investment," page 122.

railway interests in China, is amply illustrated by the various concessions contracted by British financiers in later years, especially in 1914. An authoritative text of the agreements was not available to the author, with the exception of one. The control provisions seem to be of a milder form similar to the so-called Tientsin-Pukow terms, which will be a subject of investigation in Chapter VIII. Since the fate of these railways is uncertain owing to the war, we shall only give a brief enumeration of the more important ones.

The final loan agreement of the Pukow-Sinyang Railway was concluded on Nov. 14, 1913, between the Chinese Government and the Chinese Central Railways, Ltd.[72] By Article 9, the Loan was secured by a mortgage on the railway, all lands, materials, rolling stock, buildings, etc., and the revenues. And according to Article 16, the construction and control of the railway shall be vested in the Chinese Government with a Chinese Director General and a British Engineer in Chief.

In July, 1914, an agreement for the construction of the Nanking-Pinghsiang Railway was entered into between the Chinese Government and the British and Chinese Corporation.[73]

And finally, also in July, 1914, a final agreement was signed between the Ministry of Posts and Communica-

---

[72] See "Far Eastern Review," Vol. X, page 307.
[73] See "Far Eastern Review," Vol. XI, page 49.

tions and Messrs. Pauling & Co., Ltd., of London for the construction of a railway starting from a point on the Yangtsze River opposite the city and port of Shasi, in the Province of Hupeh, through Lichow, Changteh, Shenchow, Yuanchow, Chenyuan, Kweiyang, Anshunfu to Shingyifu, in the southwestern corner of the Province of Kweichow, with a branch from Changteh to the city of Changsha, the capital of the Province of Hunan.[74] The loan is for L10,000,000 for 40 years at five per cent. interest.   The railroad is to be built by contract, a firm of British consulting engineers acting with the Chinese managing director in drawing plans and supervising the work.   The admission of Messrs. Pauling & Co. was due to a modification of British policy following the failure of the International Loan Negotiations.[75]

Succeeding chapters will incidentally, by means of comparison, further emphasize the preponderance of British finance in China, based as it is upon the wealth and the extended and old established trade relations of Great Britain, both of which — at least previous to the Great War — were superior to those of any other country.

[74] See "Far Eastern Review," Vol. xi, page 52.
[75] See Chapter VIII.

CHAPTER III

RUSSIA

RUSSIA's policy in the Far East shows a marked contrast to that of Great Britain. The causes of this contrast lie in the differences in national character and governmental system of each.[1] The administration of the Russian Empire under autocratic rule, resting nominally in the hands of the Tsar, was actually entrusted to a body of ministers and officers who were practically untrammeled in their action, and their freedom was restrained neither by the criticism of a free press, the influence of public opinion, nor the liability of being deprived of office by a parliamentary vote of censure. It follows that the Russian diplomatist was in a position to attain any object he may have had in view.

Russia has always contained statesmen who have guided her destinies along imperial lines; statesmen who have seen beyond many generations and whose grand and far-reaching policy, in spite of grievous errors in local administration, has made the Russian Empire what it was before the war. But their system was entirely opportunist, the method often without scruple. In her

[1] The first point will be dealt with at the end of this chapter.

descent on Asiatic waters Russia has been impelled neither by the need of extended territory nor by the desire for commercial relations with other countries. Indeed Russia's trade with China was and is insignificant and consists mainly of importing articles of Chinese manufacture into Russia, notably tea, silks and drugs. Her ambitions were political and her absorptions have been prompted partly by a craving for a seaboard, partly by a political instinct of expansion, and partly by the personal ambitions of a few statesmen.

It may be said that the designs of Russia in regard to China first began to take serious shape in 1854, when the celebrated Count Muravieff seized the Amur River. Although this measure of aggression may have long been in the minds of Russian statesmen, it was precipitated by reason of the blockade of the Black Sea during the Crimean War. The severance of communication by sea compelled Russia to secure control over the river as a means of conveying supplies to her distant possessions in the East. It was Muravieff himself who had first aroused public interest in the Amur, when he defended Kamchatka via this river. To quote Vladimir: " The unexpected news of the gallant defense of Petropavlofsk, a detached little-known episode of the Crimean War, an event of great importance in the Far East, aroused the greatest enthusiasm." [2] At the same time,

[2] See Vladimir, " Russia on the Pacific," page 225.

as Douglas points out: "The Anglo-French expedition of 1857–60 enabled Russia to pose as the friend of China."[3] The result was the Treaty of Aigun of May 16, 1858, strengthened by another treaty of 1860.[4] These treaties gave Russia the whole coast of Manchuria to the Korean frontier, the so-called Maritime Provinces, and provided for trade free of all duties and restrictions between Russia on the land frontiers. "This quiet transfer," says Vladimir, "was due more to the internal troubles and foreign wars of China, than to the shadowy nature of the sovereignty in the disputed territory."[5] The new territory thus acquired enabled Russia to found her great eastern seaport, Vladivostok. By the same treaty the right of Russia to retain an envoy at Peking was conceded, and from that time on to the present Russia has retained her most able diplomatists at the Celestial capital for the purpose of developing her aims and extending her interests in China.

The extension of these interests is largely connected with the building of the Siberian Railway. It had become indispensably necessary, if the acquisition of the new Far Eastern territory as well as the whole of Siberia was to bear any fruit for Russia, that cheap and rapid means of communication should be established between European Russia and the head waters of the Amur.

[3] See Douglas, "Europe and The Far East," page 190.
[4] See Mayers, op. cit., page 105.
[5] See Vladimir, op. cit., page 317.

The consequence was the construction of the Siberian Railway which Vladimir calls the "economic concomitant of Russian expansion on the Pacific.". Although originally, as far as the motives which inspired the scheme of the Siberian Railway were concerned, these may be regarded as primarily economical, there can be no doubt that the strategical advantage began to loom up in large proportions, as soon as the construction of the line through to the Pacific coast was actually undertaken in 1891. While up to this year the preoccupation of Russia in the Balkans and in Central Asia had prevented the advance of Russia south of the Amur and west of the Ussuri, she now began to give the problems of the Far East her full and undivided attention. Russia began to realize something of the immense possibilities of China, and last not least she recognized that her ambition was only partially achieved as long as she had not found a harbor entirely free from ice, Vladivostok being icebound for several months in each year. The outcome of such considerations was found in an extension of the Siberian Railway through Eastern Mongolia and Manchuria to the coast of the Yellow Sea. To this end careful surveys were made by Russian experts in Manchuria, and the possibilities of the country studied at the instance of the Russian Government.[6]

Meanwhile, Russian diplomacy was exceedingly active

[6] See Kent, op. cit., pages 40 ff.

at Peking in 1890 and 1891, and it was directed towards delaying the construction by China of the Manchurian railways projected by Li Hung Chang, in order that concessions for railways in this region should be granted to Russia. What relations between Li Hung Chang and Russia existed at this time, may perhaps never be known. He may or may not have intended from the beginning to concede these lines to Russia for a consideration.

It was so much easier for the Russians to reach their ends as Li Hung Chang, that astute Chinese statesman, though alive to Russian antagonism, shared Russia's suspicion of the Japanese and set to work to secure Russia's prospective help in his plans to thwart Japan. The trouble centering around Korea was boding ill for the peace of the Far East.[7] To Russia, China always had looked as the mighty neighbor, for Russia in her contact with the Chinese never had failed to impress the celestials with a sense of her power. Li Hung Chang acted towards Russia in a friendly spirit and treated her as a Power which, being geographically and historically quite differently situated to the rest of Europe, was worthy of different treatment.

The result of the Korean War, so disastrous to China, tightened the bonds of sympathy between Russia and China. The alarm experienced in Peking at the spec-

[7] See Douglas, op. cit., page 304.

tacle of Japanese troops overrunning Korea and the Liaotung peninsula was shared in St. Petersburg. Japan, as will be shown later, had disclosed her hand, and in doing so had stimulated Russian diplomacy to the exercise of the greatest ingenuity in order to deprive her of the substantial fruits of her victory. It was inevitable that Russia should rely on diplomatic action, for military measures were not at that time practicable. The Siberian Railway was not completed, and it would have been impossible for her to throw into Manchuria a force sufficient to effect the seizure of the Liaotung peninsula from Japan. She therefore used the Yellow Peril argument with such effect that Germany and France joined her in insisting upon the withdrawal of Japan from Port Arthur and from Korea.[8] Japan had to accept the inevitable, and to withdraw, for she could not have withstood a naval attack upon her shores by three allied powers.

It is of great significance that Li Hung Chang had accepted the Japanese conditions without demur. He had apparently previously come to an understanding with the Russian representative at Peking, by which the intervention of the Tsar was promised to prevent the permanent occupation of the Chinese territory by Japan, and he knew that the most important clause in the peace-treaty would not be allowed to be carried out. Natu-

[8] See Le Roy Beaulieu, "The Awakening of the East," page 247.

rally his gratitude towards Russia was great, and his
obligations soon resulted in a large increase of Russian
influence at Peking.[9]   During the latter part of 1895,
and the entire year of 1896, Russian diplomacy was very
busy in impressing upon the Chinese the fact that it was
Russia alone who had saved her from the fate of losing
parts of Manchuria, that closer relations with Russia
would ensure China's safety, and that a compensation
should be given to Russia in some form.

The visit of Li Hung Chang to St. Petersburg in 1895
paved the way for the striking events that were to follow
in Manchuria.[10]   Li Hung Chang was sent as Plenipo-
tentiary Extraordinary to be present at the coronation of
the Tsar in Moscow.   During his visit to Russia there
were rumors of the confirmation by him of a secret convention which had been entered into between China and
Russia in 1895, the so-called Cassini Convention.   Count
Cassini, the Russian minister to China, was said to have
had a series of interviews with the viceroy of Pechili,
with whom he negotiated a secret treaty, which was
subsequently ratified by Prince Lobanow, the Russian
minister of foreign affairs.   The alleged text of this
agreement was published in the *North China Daily*

[9] The mysteries of Li Hung Chang's relations to Russia have been
expounded in almost every important book on the Far East. Reliable official data are not available and the author has merely presented a brief summary of the situation.
[10] See Kent, op. cit., pages 46 ff.

News,[11] but official denials were at once published. Subsequent events, however, have proved that an understanding had been come to between Russia and China, which for all practical purposes was in the terms of the document published in the Shanghai *Journal.* " Putting the matter briefly, the arrangement amounted to an exchange of guarantees, Russia undertaking to support China against foreign aggression in return for certain facilities for the extension of Russian interests and the construction of railways in Manchuria." [12] In the Cassini Convention we see according to Mr. Putnam Weale the three main points of view at work, which Russia wanted China to get accustomed to: [13] " The first was that Russia, being without any convenient bases in the Far East, free from ice all the year round, must be granted some port or ports, which she could share with China. The second point, leading as it were to the third, was, that unless Russia were able to exert her great strength as a land Power her friendship with China could not take the form of material support in case a fresh crisis in the Far East should arise, and Japan attempt to repay China for calling in the help of the West. And the third and concluding point was this: In order to bring her myriads of soldiers to the Far East, Russia had

[11] See " North China Herald," October 30th, 1896, pages 739–741. A French text can be found in Cordier, op. cit., Vol. III, pages 343 ff.
[12] See Kent, op. cit., page 47.
[13] See Putnam Weale, " The Reshaping of the Far East," page 263.

already begun, years before the Japanese War, a grand trunk railway at great expense to herself; but as the railway would have to follow the northern bank of the Amur, it would be indefinitely delayed unless a more convenient route could be granted by generous and magnanimous China, who had already· bestowed the Primorsk."

The Cassini Convention, it was believed, also made some provisions in regard to the acquisition of Kiaochau by Russia, while the Liaotung Peninsula was ear-marked in Russia's favor.[14]   Russia's propositions seem to have appealed to Li Hung Chang, though it is hardly to be doubted that he fathomed the true significance of the convention.   He wanted an alliance; and the defensive alliance with Russia was the peg on which he hung the railway concession.   " Li Hung Chang, in his communications to the Chinese Government, laid all the stress upon this guarantee, stating that it was of inestimable worth to China, against whom England and Japan were hatching plots.   He treated it as the price to be paid for the railway charter, and all the other grants that were superadded to the charter." [15]

Shortly after his return to China, Li Hung Chang's arrangement with Russia began to bear fruit.   The first manifestation took the form of the Manchurian Rail-

[14] See Cordier, op. cit., pages 343 ff.
[15] Lawton, op. cit., Vol. II, page 1293.

way agreement between the Chinese Government and the Russo-Chinese Bank. This bank was destined to play a great rôle in the succeeding events and its establishment marks the beginning of Russian " conquest by railroad and bank." The original inscription bearing imperial sanction was signed, it is important to note, by the " Manager of Affairs of the Committee of the Siberian Railway." [16]   In virtue of the charter, a joint-stock company was founded with a capital, originally fixed at six million roubles — increased later. According to Part II, Article 14: " The object of the Russo-Chinese Bank is exclusively to develop relations with the East-Asiatic countries." Among the usual banking operations are: " The collection of duties in the Empire of China, and the transactions relating to the State Treasury of the respective place, the coinage, with the authorization of the Chinese Government, of the country's money, the payment of the interest on loans, concluded by the Chinese Government, the acquisition of concessions for the construction of railways within the boundaries of China and the establishment of telegraph lines."

Though the bank appears to be a private corporation under Government protection, its political aspect is quite apparent. " In addition to a banking department it has

[16] See Rockhill, op. cit., No. 31. See also Putnam Weale, " Manchu and Muscovite," page 126.

a political side, to which the former is said to be sub-
ordinated." [17]

On Sept. 8, 1896, the Russo-Chinese Bank entered
into an agreement with the Chinese Government for the
construction and management of the Chinese Eastern
Railway.[18] The principal provisions, establishing Russian control, are as follows:

In Article 1: "China and Russia establish a Company to be called the Chinese Eastern Railway Co. to
construct and manage this Railway. . . . The regulations of the Company will be in conformity with those
of Russian Railway Companies. Shares may only be
bought by Chinese and Russians."

In Article 6: "As regards the land required by the
Company for constructing, managing, and protecting
the line and adjacent land, for procuring sand, earth,
stones and lime, if the land be government land, it will be
given the Company without payment. . . . All the Company's land will be exempted from land tax. As soon
as the land comes under the management of the Company, they may erect thereon any buildings and carry on
all kinds of work, they may establish a telegraph line
thereon worked by the Company for the Company's
use."

Article 7: "All materials required by the Company

17 See Kent, op. cit., page 47.
18 See Rockhill, op. cit., No. 32.

for the construction and repair of the line will be exempt from taxation."

In Article 8: "All Russian troops, naval or military, and munitions of war, moved by the Russian Government by this Railway, must be conveyed by the Company directly across the border."

In Article 10: "As to goods conveyed by this line from Russia to China or from China to Russia, they will pay duty according to the Treaty Tariff, i.e., an Import or Export duty as the case may be, but subject to a reduction of one-third of the Tariff rate."

On the strength of this agreement the "Chinese Eastern Railway Company" was formed " for the construction and working of a railway within the confines of China from one of the points on the western borders of the Provinces of Hei-Lun-Tsian, to one of the points on the eastern borders of the Province of Kirin and for the connection of this railway with those branches which the Imperial Russian Government will construct to the Chinese frontier from Trans-Baikalia and the southern Ussuri lines." [19]   The Company is, furthermore, empowered, subject to the sanction of the Chinese Government, to exploit, in connection with the railway or independently of it, coal mines, as also to exploit in China other enterprises — mining, industrial, and commercial. The formation of the Company shall be undertaken by the

[19] See Rockhill, op. cit., No. 33.

Russo-Chinese Bank. With the formation of the Company all rights and obligations are transferred to it in regard to the construction and working of the line ceded in virtue of the above named Agreement of the 8th of September, 1896. In virtue of this Agreement the Company shall retain possession of the Chinese Eastern Railway during the course of eighty years from the day of the opening of traffic along the whole line. But on the expiration of thirty-six years the Chinese Government has the right of acquiring the line. The railway is to be conducted subservient to the requirements of the Siberian Railway. In the event of a difference of opinion arising between the two railways the Chinese Eastern Railway shall submit to the decision of the Russian Minister of Finances. The Russian letter and parcels post, as also the officials accompanying the same, shall be carried by the Chinese Eastern Railway free of charge. The preservation of law and order on the lands assigned to the railway and its appurtenances shall be confined to police agents appointed by the Company. The capital of the Company shall be formed by the issue of shares and bonds. The shares shall be fixed at 5,000,000 rubles. The remaining portion of the capital of the Company will be formed by the issue of bonds. The nominal amount and value of each issue of bonds shall be subject to the sanction of the Minister of Finances. The Russian Government will guarantee the interest on and amortization of the bonds. For the realization of these bonds the Company must have recourse to the Russo-Chinese Bank.

The character of " control " established by the foregoing agreements can easily be ascertained. The fact that according to Article 1 of the last agreement " the Director of the Company will be appointed by China," and that " his duty will be to supervise the task delegated to the Company by China, and to ascertain whether his obligations are faithfully performed," does not alter the fact that the Company is a Russian joint stock company, run by Russians, with Russian money, and under Russian rules. One of the points, which is emphasized by Kent, is that " no person except of Chinese or Russian nationality could become a shareholder, which meant, of course, a purely Russian company, for . . . the Chinese had not reached that stage of education when the idea of joint-stock enterprise either inspires confidence or appears attractive." [20]   And Kent continues: " In this company, which was to be known and ultimately came into existence as the Chinese Eastern Railway Company, the sole control of the line was vested, and also rights, in connection with the railway, and independently of it, of mineral, industrial, and commercial exploitation."

But in addition to the fact that this railway company

[20] See Kent, op. cit., page 48.

is of Russian ownership, we have to bear in mind, that the control over the owners is exercised by the Russo-Chinese Bank, a state-controlled institution. To justify this contention it would not even be necessary to ascertain who the owners of the shares are. It appears to us, on the strength of all " control " provisions, as self-evident that the road is state-controlled and that Russian control in China is of a political nature. To disperse any doubt about the nature of Russian control we shall support our contention by the following considerations: Comparing the Russian control provisions with those to be found in the British agreements we find that no protection is made for the shareholders, who are the nominal owners. There is no mortgage on the railway, because there is no loan made to the Chinese Government. Only the bondholders are protected, namely, by a Russian Government guarantee! The management rests permanently with the company, though nominally under Chinese supervision. In fact all control provisions characteristic of English agreements are absent. This fact, however, would in itself not be sufficient to prove the political character of Russia's control. Nominally, Russian control remains financial, since the contracts containing the respective provisions are on the Russian side concluded by private citizens and since the object of the contracts is a financial proposition, namely the building of a railroad. But what we are interested in, is the spirit of the control provisions, and not their wording.

The political and military character of the railway is manifested in the railroad police, or so-called railroad guards. These were Russian soldiers and they formed a small army. These guards and the so-called railroad " zones," i.e., lands granted to the company upon which settlements were established under Russian administrations, will be an object of our investigation at a later occasion.

As a further support of our contention we shall quote Kent once more. Referring to the two points between which the railroad was to run, Kent remarks: " In other words, permission was given to continue the Trans-Siberian line across Manchuria to Vladivostok instead of following the more circuitous route along the Amur, which presented almost insurmountable difficulties to railroad construction." [21] The new railway through Chinese territory is, indeed, nothing else than part and parcel of the Trans-Siberian Railroad, which is owned and controlled by the Russian Government. Its purpose is mainly strategical. Such is at least the opinion of the British representative in China, Sir C. MacDonald, who wrote in 1898: " The Manchurian Railway Concession dates from 1896. As is well known, it was obtained as recompense for help given in securing the

[21] See Kent, op. cit., page 48.

retrocession of Liaotung. . . . The concession is purely strategical." [22]

The agreement enabled Russia to dispense with the originally projected line along the north bank of the Amur, gave the Russians the permission of continuing the Trans-Siberian line across Manchuria to Vladivostok, and also prepared the way for further extensions southwards. In other words, the Manchurian Railway enabled Russia to dominate the whole of North Manchuria.

The construction of the Chinese Eastern Railway was begun in 1897. Meanwhile diplomacy appears to have been active in preparing for the southern extension of the line towards the Gulf of Chili in order to secure a post which should be free from the disadvantage which attached to Vladivostok of being annually icebound for several months. Events again facilitated and hastened Russian movements. Germany had compelled the Chinese Government to give a lease of the region around Kiaochau Bay for ninety-nine years. It has been suggested that China was under promise to grant Russia a concession in the Kiaochau region,[23] and that Russia embraced the opportunity of the grant to Germany to insist upon a lease of the Liaotung peninsula, including the harbor and fortress of Port Arthur, for twenty-five

[22] See "China," No. 1, 1899, Vol. CIX, No. 459, Enclosure 2.
[23] See below, page 86.

years, and upon the right to construct a railway to connect Port Arthur with the Chinese Eastern Railway. The lease of the Liaotung peninsula was granted on the 27th of March, 1898, including the right to build a railway connecting Port Arthur with Harbin, and another connecting Talienwan (later Dalny and now called Dairen by the Japanese) with Newchwang.[24] The eighth clause provided for a branch of the railway southward: "The Chinese Government agree that the principle of the permission given in the twenty-second year of Kuang Hsu (1896) to the Manchurian Railway Company for the construction of a railway shall now, from the date of signature, be extended to the construction of a branch line from a certain station on the aforesaid main line to Talienwan, or, if necessity requires, the same principle shall be extended to the construction of a branch line from the main line to a convenient point on the seacoast in the Liaotung Peninsula, between Yingtzu (Nuochwang) and the Yalu River. The provisions of the agreement of the 8th of September, 1896, between the Chinese Government and the Russo-Chinese Bank shall be strictly observed with regard to the branch line above mentioned. The direction of the line and the places it is to pass shall be arranged by Hsu-Ta-jen and the Manchurian Railway Company." The article ends with the important proviso that " this railway concession is

[24] See Rockhill, op. cit., Nos. 9 and 10.

never to be used as a pretext for encroachment on Chinese territory, nor to be allowed to interfere with Chinese authority, or interests." Article III of the Additional Agreement, signed at St. Petersburg on the 7th of May, 1898, provides that the terminus of the line should be at Port Arthur and Talienwan. It is further agreed in common that railway privileges in districts traversed by this branch line shall not be given to the subjects of other Powers.

" Russia having gained her points, the Russification of the country proceeded fast. Port Arthur was fortified, a modern town built at Dalny, and railway construction pushed on. The line was now divided into three sections: the Western, from the Siberian frontier to Harbin; the Eastern, from Harbin to Vladivostok; and the Southern, consisting of the branch from Harbin to Port Arthur. The paramount importance of the last-named, in Russian eyes, was soon made manifest, for though the eastern and western section received merely ordinary attention, the Port Arthur branch was pushed on with the utmost dispatch. . . . The gauge adopted for the line was five feet, the Russian standard, which was especially stipulated for in the agreement in order that it might be uniform with the Trans-Siberian Road. So rapidly was the work pushed on, that by the time of the Boxer outbreak the line was almost through." [25]

[25] See Kent, op. cit., page 50.

The railway could be opened to traffic in 1901. "Control" over the road is absolutely identical to that over the North Manchurian line. For the railway is merely a branch line of the Chinese Eastern Railway, and is thus subject to all the agreements referring to the latter, as explicitly stipulated in Article 8 of the convention of March 27, 1898. The whole Manchurian Railway places Russia in the possession of a direct route to Peking and at once gives her a predominance in Northern China, which places other powers at a marked disadvantage.

It was especially the British colony in China that was worried about Russia's activity in the north. The China Association wrote on April 14, 1898, to Lord Salisbury: "The Association feels no confidence that the door of Manchuria will be left open by the Great Power which has obtained possession of lock, bolt, and bar. An ice-free port was a necessary concession to its commercial needs. The fact that that port has taken the form of a fortress, which can be rendered practically impregnable, violently changes the situation." [26]

But it is also important to notice the Russian point of view. In an Official Communication of the Russian Official Messenger of March, 1898, we read in reference to the lease of Port Arthur and the Russian railway rights in Manchuria: "This Agreement is a direct and

[26] See "China," No. 1, 1899, Vol. CIX, No. 25.

natural outcome of the friendly relations between great
neighboring Empires, all of whose endeavors should be
directed towards the preservation of tranquillity along
the vast extent of their neighboring possessions for the
common benefit of the people of both of them. . . .
Securing the inviolability of the sovereign rights of
China, and satisfying the daily requirements of Russia
in her capacity of a great and neighboring naval Power,
this Agreement can in no way injure the interests of any
other Power; on the contrary, it gives to all nations of
the world the possibility in the near future of entering
into communication with this hitherto closed-up country
on the coast of the Yellow Sea." [27]

English objections to Russia's Manchurian enterprises
were severely criticized by the Russian Press, to judge
from extracts given in the British Blue Books.[28]   The
Novosti says for instance that "Russia's recent action
in the Far East meets with the sympathy of all countries
excepting England.   This shows how thoroughly the
majority of foreign Powers believes in the sincerity of
Russia's desire for peace.   England, who always opposed Russia's lawful aspirations, would obstruct her
now were she not happily isolated. . . . At present England is helpless before Russia, because the latter is supported by France and Germany.   There is no formal

[27] See " China," No. 1, 1899, Vol. CIX, No. 1.
[28] See " China," No. 1, 1899, Vol. CIX, No. 14, Enclosures.

agreement between these three Powers, but there is a complete solidarity between them."

England's isolation mentioned here, led eventually to the conclusion of the Anglo-Japanese alliance. But meantime the Russian and English Governments had long discussions in reference to railway enterprises in Manchuria.[29] The British and Chinese Corporation had entered into a preliminary agreement with the Chinese Government on the 7th of June, 1898, for a sterling loan of 16,000,000 taels " for the construction of a rail-way-line from Chunghowsou to Hsinmintung, and a branch line to Ying-tzu, and for the redemption of existing loans to the Tientsin-Shanhaikwan and Tientsin-Lukouchiao lines. The security for the loan shall be the permanent way, rolling-stock, and entire property. . . . In the event of default or arrears in payment of interest or repayments of principal, the said railway lines . . . shall be handed over to representatives deputed by the Syndicate, to manage them on their behalf, until principal and interest of the loan are redeemed in full, when the management will revert to the Railway Administration."[30] Whereupon the Russian Representative in China protested against the arrangement, and especially against the provision of British control in case of default. A long series of negotiations followed, until

[29] A detailed account of these is given by Kent, op. cit., pages 51 ff.
[30] See Rockhill, op. cit., No. 42.

finally a compromise was reached, which is expressed in Article 4 of the final agreement of Oct. 10, 1898.[31] " This arrangement, which differs from other contracts in that the Administrator-General retains control of the railway lines so long as the principal and interest of this loan are regularly paid, has been agreed to in consequence of the friendly relations which have long existed between the Contracting Parties." Sic!

The ultimate outcome of the Russo-British negotiations was the official recognition of the respective " spheres of interest " as quoted in Chapter II. A supplementary note recorded the understanding arrived at in respect to the Shanhaikuan Newchwang section of the Imperial Railways of North China.

While Russia thus excluded England from railway participation in her sphere, England was not able to exclude Russia entirely from hers. It had been Russia's great desire to secure control of a railway from the north which would join with a line from Indo-China, and to establish a through trunk route bisecting China and under control of Russia and her ally France. But bound by the agreement with England, she could only accomplish her ends through the medium of a third party. This Russia apparently did by entrusting her interests to others. She retired into the background, and confided the

[31] The correspondence between the British and Russian Governments with regard to Railway interests in Manchuria are contained in " China," No. 2, 1899, Vol. CIX.

active work of advancing her interests to her allies and financial agents, France and Belgium.

In 1897 a Belgian syndicate obtained a concession for a line from Peking to Hankow. The hand of Russia in the negotiations was clearly seen. In Article 18 [32] it was stipulated that the Russo-Chinese Bank would be the agent for the bonds, and Article 20 provided that the Russo-Chinese Bank should be the bank of deposit and the medium for monthly payments. The British Government soon realized the significance of the Belgian venture and did not entertain any illusions as to the real character of the Belgian concessions. At the time the agreement was ready to be signed, Sir Claude Mac-Donald raised the strongest objection.[33] His principal criticism of the contract was that there was no security against the railway's transfer to a bank or syndicate of another nationality (namely Russian), that there is withdrawn from Chinese control all concern with the construction of the line, and all power of interference with the selection of the employees and the fixing of the rates and that the Russian Minister, together with the French and Belgian, was to be the judge in certain disputes; while his principal objection was directed against any participation of the Russo-Chinese Bank.[34] Any British objection, however, proved to be without avail, for China

[32] See Rockhill, op. cit., No. 34.
[33] See Chapter II.
[34] See "China," No. 1, 1899, Vol. CIX, No. 347.

seemed to have been determined and Russian pressure seemed to have been stronger than British demonstrations.

The arrangement was embodied in two documents, a loan contract and an operating contract.[35] The latter confers wide powers of management upon the syndicate, and gives them complete financial control of the line. Article I provides as follows: " The Chinese Railway Company (represented by the Viceroys of Chili and Hupeh) in accord with the Imperial Chinese Government, entrusts the Société d'Étude de Chemins de Fer en Chine (the Belgian syndicate) which shall appoint representatives for that purpose, with the direction, administration, and operating of the line from Hankow to Peking." According to Article II, " The Société d'Étude or the representatives of it shall appoint . . . shall organize the various services, shall have the right to hire the personnel, which it shall have absolute right to dismiss, or disband, and to fix its salaries according to a fixed schedule previously communicated to the Director General of the Chinese Railway Company. It shall make all purchases necessary for operating, maintaining or repairing the road, it shall fix the schedule of rates in the terms of concession contracts, collect revenues of all kinds and pay the operating and management expenses of the Company."

[35] See Rockhill, op. cit., No. 34.

The loan itself is secured by a mortgage on the railway, rolling stock, etc.   In short, the control provisions are in substance identical to those embodied in the English contracts; for we have to remember that the English control provisions were explicitly shaped after the Belgian contract.[36]   In other words, the Belgian control provisions are financial in nature.   Yet their ultimate political purpose can hardly be denied.

Later railways contracted or earmarked by the Belgian syndicate tended further to strengthen England's suspicions of Russia's political aims.   " The significant point is," says the *Far Eastern Review,* " that the last performance of this Company brings into effect the identical scheme which the Russians long ago cherished to obtain railway domination in certain spheres in China." [37] The lines referred to as secured by the Belgian company are a continuation of the Trans-Caspian System of Russia through Sinkiang (Chinese Turkestan) and Kansu, and leading from Lanchow to Sian, Honan, Kaifeng to the sea.   The other Belgian project is a line longitudinally through the province of Shansi and is to connect the above mentioned line with the Peking-Kalgan extension, a Russian venture, at Tatungfu.   The company has the option to extend this railway in the south to Chengtu, the capital of Szechuan.

[36] See Chapter II.
[37] See " Far Eastern Review," Vol. 10, pages 92 and 290.

To this the *Far Eastern Review* remarks: "No railways in China are likely to have such an important bearing, however, upon the political future of the country as these two routes which have now come under the dominance of the Belgian financial organization. Apart from its political bearing, however, the projected railway will place in the hands of the Belgian syndicate the greatest amount of mileage held by any individual nation in China, and the two routes will embrace an area of country of tremendous importance to Russia, whose financiers are alleged to be interested in the Compagnie Générale de Chemins de Fer et de Tramways en Chine. Considered from a purely economic standpoint the proposed line is likely to have a tremendous influence upon the development of one of the richest mineral-bearing provinces of China." [38]

Our discourse on the Belgian schemes, though apparently a diversion from our theme, was to illustrate Russian political designs in the Far East. Aside from the improbability of an early construction of these railways as a result of the war, and a consequent lack of practical value, the fact that the text of the agreements was not available to the author makes it inadvisable, if not impossible, to go into further details.

The political character of Russian railways in China, at least previous to the Russo-Japanese War, is most ap-

[38] See "Far Eastern Review," Vol. 10, page 89.

parent in Manchuria. Here events were favorable for further attempts at advance. In 1900 the Boxer disturbances threw the whole of North China into chaos; and Russia immediately occupied Manchuria, ostensibly to secure the maintenance of order. Newchwang and Mukden were occupied and a military occupation was regularly instituted along the whole Russian railway in Manchuria.[39]   Any intentions of a Russian occupation however were repeatedly denied by the Russian minister to China.[40]   Nevertheless Europe continued to be alarmed at Russian activities and the Anglo-German convention of Oct. 16, 1900, was a direct outcome of the Manchurian situation.[41]   Its main object was to restrain any power which might be disposed to violate the principle of equal opportunity in China or her territorial integrity.

Meanwhile the Powers were occupied with settling the questions arising out of the Boxer rebellion. After the legations had been relieved by the international expeditionary force, the Powers proceeded to negotiate with China upon the terms under which they would evacuate Peking. Until a general treaty was concluded between China and the coöperating Powers, it was obvious that it would be at least inappropriate for any individual power to seek to negotiate a separate treaty with China.

[39] See " China," No. 1, 1901, Vol. XCI, No. 391.
[40] See " China," No. 1, 1901, XCI, Nos. 234, 256, and others.
[41] See Rockhill, op. cit., No. 14.

But early in 1901 the news came out, of a draft of an agreement into which China was supposed to have entered with Russia respecting Manchuria. At the inquiry by Japan and England of the Russian and Chinese Governments as to the existence of the alleged convention, both governments kept a strict silence. Whereupon China was warned by Great Britain, Germany, Japan and the United States against entering into a separate agreement with one power while it was negotiating for peace with all powers collectively.[42] Strongly pressed by the powers, China finally communicated the text of the agreement and asked immediately thereafter the respective Foreign Offices to mediate between her and Russia.[43]

The principal terms of the Agreement were:[44] Manchuria to be restored; Assistance to be given to China by Russia in keeping order; No army to be maintained by China until the completion of the Manchurian railway. The strength of the police is to be settled with Russia; they are not to possess artillery, and no foreigners other than Russians are to be employed in it; Abolition of Chinese administration in the town of Chinchou. China is not to grant any mining, railway or other rights without the permission of Russia in the territory upon the Russian border, i.e., Manchuria, Mon-

[42] See " China," No. 6, 1901, Vol. CXI, Nos. 79 and 106.
[43] See " China," No. 6, 1901, Vol. CXI, No. 137.
[44] See " China," No. 6, 1901, Vol. CXI, No. 130.

golia, Ili, Yarkand, etc., and Russia's permission is to be obtained before China builds railways in these. With reference to the damages suffered by the Manchurian Railway these shall be made good. . . . Instead of this, concessions may be accepted or existing contracts modified. Until the last provisions are carried out, Russia will maintain an additional force for the protection of the Manchurian Railway!

This agreement shows better than anything else the true ambitions of Russia in the Far East and the kind of control she desired to exercise — if it had not been for Japan. Russia's duplicity during and after the Boxer troubles may be illustrated by a quotation from Putnam Weale: " During 1901, Russia had three distinct and separate rôles to play in China: the part of ally to all Europe; the part of China's dear and secret friend in Peking; and the part of Manchuria's real master in the invaded provinces; whilst over and above in Europe she had to quiet the secret fears of numerous Chancelleries busily inquiring as to her real plans in the future." [45]

Backed by the support of the Powers, China refused to sign and Russia withdrew temporarily.[46] Then followed the Anglo-Japanese alliance; whereupon Russia modified her demands in respect to Manchuria. On April 8, 1902, an agreement was concluded between Rus-

[45] See Putnam Weale, " Reshaping of the Far East," page 263.
[46] See " China," No. 6, 1901, Vol. CXI, No. 238.

sia and China containing the following principal terms.[47]
Manchuria was to be restored to the Chinese Government; but China was to observe strictly the stipulations
of the contract concluded with the Russo-Chinese Bank
in 1896. Russia was to withdraw her troops gradually
from Manchuria. Russia agrees to restore to the owners the Railway Shanhaikuan-Newchwang-Sinmintung.
No other Power shall be allowed to participate in this
railroad in any form nor to occupy the territory evacu-
ated. Should extension of the line be contemplated,
the Russian Government was to be consulted first; expenses for repair and working of said line were to be paid
by China.

The Russians did not observe these terms faithfully;
on the contrary, they established themselves more firmly
at the mouth of the Liao River.[48] The diplomacy of
Russia was accompanied by hurried exploitation on the
part of Russian speculators of the valuable timber region of the Yalu River, by encroachments upon Korea,
and by enormous expenditures at Dalny, which the Russians destined for a great port. In these adventures
and in the neglect of military precautions, Russia was
simply playing the game of Japan and hastening the moment when this Power was to take over Russia's railway
rights in South Manchuria.

[47] See " China," No. 2, 1904, Vol. CX, page 36 ff. See also Rockhill, op. cit., No. 17.
[48] See " China," No. 2, 1904, Vol. CX, page 63.

The Treaty of Portsmouth of Aug. 23rd, 1905, deprived Russia of the southern part of the Manchurian Railway.[49] Article VI says: " The Imperial Russian Government engages to transfer and assign to the Imperial Government of Japan, without compensation and with the assent of the Chinese Government, the railway between Changchun (Kuanchengtzu) and Port Arthur and all its branches together with all rights, privileges, and properties appertaining thereto in that region, as well as all coal mines in the said region belonging to or worked for the benefit of the railway."— The consent of the Chinese Government was, of course, forthcoming.— According to article VII Japan and Russia engage to exploit their respective railways in Manchuria " exclusively for commercial and industrial purposes and in no wise for strategic purposes." Article III stipulates: " Japan and Russia mutually engage, (1) To evacuate completely and simultaneously Manchuria except the territory affected by the lease of the Liaotung Peninsula, in conformity with the provisions of additional Article I annexed to this Treaty; and (2) To restore entirely and completely to the exclusive administration of China all portions of Manchuria now in the occupation or under the control of the Japanese or Russian troops, with the exception of the territory above mentioned. The Imperial Government of Russia declares that they have not

[49] See " British and Foreign State Papers," Vol. 98, page 735.

in Manchuria any territorial advantages or preferential or exclusive concessions in impairment of Chinese sovereignty or inconsistent with the principle of equal opportunity." And in Article V: " The Imperial Russian Government transfers and assigns to the Imperial Governmment of Japan, with the consent of the Government of China, the lease of Port Arthur, Talien, and adjacent territory and territorial waters and all rights, privileges, and concessions connected with or forming part of such lease, and they also transfer and assign to the Imperial Government of Japan all public works and properties in the territory affected by the above-mentioned lease."

In other words, the Treaty of Portsmouth deprived Russia of her strategical stronghold in South Manchuria, of her railway rights in said region, and checked any possible Russian ambitions at political control of all Manchuria. Russian control in the Russian " sphere " i.e., in North Manchuria, could therefore — legally — be based exclusively upon the railway agreements between the Russo-Chinese Bank, respectively the Chinese Eastern Railway Company and the Chinese Government. The control provisions have been analyzed above and the character and degree of control been stated. Two aspects of Russian control in Manchuria, however, remain to be investigated: the railway guards and the railway zones. As to the first point the writer has to acknowledge his inability to secure accurate figures as to the number of soldiers employed. The amount has been constantly varying and the figures found in the literature appear most unreliable. The figure is large or small according to the sympathies or antipathies of the writers. The supplementary agreement to the Treaty of Portsmouth provides, that " within a period of eighteen months from that date (i.e., immediately after the Treaty of Peace comes into operation) the armies of the two countries shall be completely withdrawn from Manchuria except from the leased territory of the Liaotung Peninsula."

The Russian title to railway " zones " in North Manchuria is based upon Article VI of the Russo-Chinese Bank's treaty with China of Sept. 8, 1896.[50]   The respective phrases read as follows: " As regards the land required by the Company for constructing, managing, and protecting the line and adjacent land, . . . it will be given the Company without payment. . . . As soon as the land comes under the management of the Company, they may erect thereon any buildings and carry on all kinds of work." . . . Lawton, however, informs us that the French text reads quite differently: " La Société aura le droit absolu et exclusif de l'administration de les terrains." [51]   On the strength of these clauses, Russia

[50] See Rockhill, op. cit., No. 32.
[51] See Lawton, " Empires of the Far East," Vol. I, page 1303.

founded townships such as Harbin and Tsitsihar, which were under Russian administration, together with all other settlements and all the extensive tracts of lands held by the Company. China objected to the extensive administrative powers exercised by Russia, until the dispute was finally settled by an agreement of May 10th, 1909.

According to Harrison, " The last agreement between the Russian and Chinese Governments arose out of the protest of the Chinese Government against that part of the 1896 Treaty which bears upon the introduction of public administration in Harbin and other settlements of the railway zone. In a strictly legal sense, China had a very weak case, and Russia's consent to the new arrangement was in the nature of a concession, but one which is to be welcomed as creating a wholesome precedent in the direction of a wider recognition of China's sovereign rights within her own territory, the true reason for the original grant of special privileges being plain enough." [52]

The agreement is simply an appendix to the railway agreement of 1896. To use the text,[53] " In view of the mutual misunderstandings which have arisen in the interpretation of the contract for the construction and working of the Chinese Eastern Railway, dated 27th of August, 1896, on consideration of the question of the organization and introduction of public administra-

[52] See Harrison, " Peace or War East of Baikal? " page 199.
[53] See " British and Foreign State Papers," Vol. 102, page 396.

tion on the lands of the Railway, the Governments of Russia and China have established the following general rules:

1. On the lands of the Chinese Eastern Railway, as a fundamental principle, are recognized the sovereign rights of China, which must not be prejudiced in any way.

2. All sovereign rights of China on the lands of the Chinese Eastern Railway are exercised by China, and neither the administration of the Railway nor public administrations shall under any pretext obstruct the exercise of these rights, if such do not infringe any of the treaties which have been concluded by the Chinese Eastern Railway Company.

3. All the treaties of the Chinese Eastern Railway at present in operation remain as before in full force.

6. On the lands of the Chinese Eastern Railway Company in settlements which possess commercial importance public administration shall be formed. The inhabitants of these settlements, in conformity with the commercial importance of a given settlement and the number of its population, shall elect delegates who, in their turn, shall choose an Executive Committee, or the inhabitants themselves shall directly superintend public affairs and elect from their number one representative who shall carry into effect the resolutions of the general assembly.

7. On the lands of the Chinese Eastern Railway Com-

pany, both the Chinese and foreign population enjoy the same rights and assume the same obligations, without the slightest difference between them.

8. All inhabitants who own a certain amount of immovable property or pay a certain annual rental and established taxes enjoy the right of participation in the election of delegates.

9. The President is elected by the Assembly of Delegates from their midst, irrespective of nationality.

10. All matters which concern the management and good order of the settlements are subject to the jurisdiction of the Assembly of Delegates, etc., etc.

11. The Assembly of Delegates elects from its midst, irrespective of nationality, members of the Executive Committee.   Their number must not be more than three. Besides this, the President of the Tsiao-she-tsui (Chinese Railway Bureau) and the President of the Railway appoint one delegate each.   The members of election and the delegates together with their President constitute the Executive Committee.

12. The President of the Assembly of Delegates is at the same time President of the Executive Committee.

13. The President of the Tsiao-she-tsui and the President of the Railway, occupying a position higher than that of the President of the Assembly of Delegates and Executive Committee, are invested with the power of

control and the right of personal revision, which they exercise when this is deemed to be indispensable, etc., etc.

14. In the event of the disagreement of the President of the Tsiao-she-tsui or the President of the Railway with the resolutions of the Assembly of Delegates, these must be transferred to the Assembly for additional investigation. Its resolution shall be deemed binding if it is passed by three-fourths of the votes of members present at the sitting of the Assembly.

15. Important public and financial questions arising in the settlements of the expropriated Zone of the Railway, on consideration by the Assembly of Delegates, are transferred to the President of the Tsiao-she-tsui and to the administration of the Chinese Eastern Railway for joint consideration and confirmation.

16. Lands which have been allotted specially for the needs of the Railway are subject to the independent control of the Chinese Eastern Railway, i.e., for stations, workshops, and so forth, etc.

In commenting in a very favorable way upon the provisions of this agreement as not establishing special privileges for Russia and as not being materially different from the privileges enjoyed in any other international settlements such as Tientsin, Shanghai and others, Harrison says: " The Russian position is made all the more impregnable in the light of the perfect freedom which every other Power enjoys to establish, if it so wishes, its own settlements at Harbin. Hitherto, however, no effort has apparently been made to take advantage of this right, and all foreigners, with singular unanimity, prefer to live in the Russian settlement." [54] And further: " Happily, it now seems probable that the Powers will yield on the point of municipal administration, it being clearly stipulated on Russia's part that she does not claim any right of legal jurisdiction over the persons of foreign subjects resident in the Russian settlement of Harbin or elsewhere within the railway zone. Extraterritoriality obtains at Harbin, as it does elsewhere throughout China, and though the Russian police may arrest a foreigner caught in flagrante delicto, they must at once surrender him to his consul for trial." [55]

Extraterritoriality and the legal status of international settlements however are not the object of our investigation. We have given a lengthy quotation from the latest Russo-Chinese railway zone agreement to prove our contention that the post-bellum control exercised by Russia in China is — legally — non-political. Though Russia may or may not have had an ultimate absorption of North Manchuria in view, the Russian control exercised in North Manchuria is strictly based upon the railway agreements including the supplementary interpreta-

[54] See Harrison, op. cit., page 201.
[55] See Harrison, op. cit., page 204.

tion of the agreements to be found in the agreement of 1909.

" The spirit which animated the Russian side of the negotiations for the agreement concluded with China on the 10th of May, 1909, was indeed so conciliatory that the Chinese at first suspected therein some deep-laid and sinister designs. The high-handed methods of the autocratic Russian Railway Company were replaced by a sweet reasonableness which the Peking Government were quite unable to understand, but of which they soon proceeded to take every advantage. No sooner had they realized that Russia was prepared to allow the exercise of their sovereign rights in the Manchurian Railway settlements, than they proceeded to encourage American and German ambitions, sedulously fomenting differences at Harbin, Khailar, and other places, by which means they hoped to obtain full administrative control of the municipalities." Such are the words of Mr. Bland, when commenting on Russia's post-bellum attitude.[56]   Harrison uses a similar language : " Russia was inclined to be too self-assertive before the war, and the inevitable nemesis overtook her : to-day, on the other hand, her representatives appear to have gone to the other extreme, with the result that Russian vested interests are in danger of being seriously jeopardized." [57]

[56] See Bland, op. cit., page 336.
[57] See Harrison, op. cit., page 209.

Of course during the evacuation period, Russia was rather slow in handing the sovereign rights over North Manchuria back to China. "Russians seem to have watched the Japanese and followed their lead in political matters. As the Japanese armies were withdrawn, so also, in about the same ratio, were the Russian armies removed from China's provinces." [58] The same writer continues: "In one important matter, however, Russia's post-bellum policy in Manchuria differed from that of Japan. This is in commercial affairs. The Russians never have pursued a niggardly policy in regard to the trade of other nations in Manchuria. On the contrary, during the Russian régime before the war foreign trade in the country greatly increased, especially that of the United States, owing to the fact that a condition of comparative order prevailed, and that the Russians interposed no obstacles to commerce. The present industrial situation of Russia does not require special exploitation in her favor of eastern markets. . . . After the war, Russia resumed this policy which was more sharply thrown into relief because of Japan's opposite attitude in the south. Russia made no attempt to prevent foreigners from entering the country after peace was established. Instead of interposing obstacles, to the importation of products, as Japan did in her sphere, Rus-

[58] See Millard, "America and the Far Eastern Question," page 276.

sian officials smoothed their way by providing routes of access."

But while the control exercised by Russia in Manchuria, of late, was very moderate, she nevertheless strengthened her position considerably by new railway enterprises in these regions. In the agreements of July 30th, 1907, July 4th, 1910, and July 3rd, 1916, Japan and Russia mutually guarantee their vested and future interests in their respective spheres and promise each other support in case of foreign interference.[59] The agreements suggest that Japan and Russia have made up their minds, eventually to divide Manchuria between them, and the first fruits of these agreements are to be seen in several new railroad contracts as well as in the effective exclusion of other powers.

Russia had, immediately after the war, begun calmly to conduct surveys in the provinces of Amur and Baikalia with a view to providing for the regeneration of Russian policy in the Far East by means of a colossal railway undertaking — the Amur Railway. A provision for connection of the Amur Railway at Blagoveshchensk was made in 1914 by means of a new Manchurian railway contract. A detailed account of this contract cannot be given for the same reasons which hindered us from investigating any other railway agreements con-

[59] The agreements will be analyzed in Chapter VI, since they are of greater importance to Japan than to Russia.

cluded within the last three years. We take our information on the project from the *Far Eastern Review,* which says: [60] " An important agreement was signed in Peking on March 27th last between the Russo-Asiatic Bank, represented by Mr. L. de Hoyer, and the Chinese Government, represented by Mr. Liang Tung-yen, the Minister of Communications, and Mr. Chou Hsu-shih, Minister of Finance, for the construction of a railway connecting the cities of Harbin, Mergen, Aigun, and Tsitsihar, in Northern Manchuria. Harbin is at the junction of the Siberian Railway and the line running south to Changchun and thence to Dalny, while Tsitsihar is connected with the Siberian Railway by a light line which will be taken over under the agreement just signed. Mergen is a little more than half way between Tsitsihar and Aigun, which is on the Amur River. North of Aigun, on the opposite side of the Amur, is the city of Blagoveshchensk, which the new railway is destined to serve. Connection will be made by means of ferry boats with what is now the village of Heiheifu, opposite Blagoveshchensk, where the railway will terminate. The total length of the proposed railway is approximately 1,000 kilometers. It will link up the Siberian Railway with the Amur River, and will consolidate Russian interests, and incidentally develop great areas of valuable territory, in North Manchuria. An inter-

[60] See " Far Eastern Review," Vol. 11, pages 150 and 385.

esting point is that it will cover the northern section of what is known as the Chinchow-Aigun project, the agreement for which is held by the American group of bankers, but which was rendered void by the energetic protests of Japan that the proposed line would parallel the South Manchuria Railroad.

" The agreement is for a loan of 50 million roubles, and an additional amount which might be required to complete the project. The loan is to be floated when financial conditions may permit after the war, and in whatever markets the Russo-Asiatic Bank may deem money to be available. The agreement is regarded as an improvement on other railway agreements in China where the interest of the financiers are concerned with control of expenditure, etc., while the Chinese Government gains a distinct pecuniary advantage owing to an arrangement being made whereby the working of exchange cannot be so disastrous as in the case of other railroad lines. . . . The bondholders receive ample protection in the usual way by having the line, etc., as security, by the employment of qualified engineers and accountants, etc., and in addition by the arrangement that the earnings of the railway shall be deposited in branches of the Russo-Asiatic Bank."

Furthermore Russia demands from China a concession for a railway from Kiakhta to Urga and through Mongolia to Kalgan, which is to connect the Siberian system with Peking via the Peking-Kalgan line. But this project is of the future.[61] Another project, namely, for a railway from Kokand, the terminus of the Central Asian line, through Kashgar, Hami, Soochow, to Lanchow-fu, in China, has also been set aside for Russia to finance and construct.[62] These lines would be purely for the advancement of Russia's strategical position in Mongolia and China, and would bring the northwest and western provinces within the Russian sphere.

The first steps towards the establishment of a Russian sphere, if not a Russian protectorate, have been taken under the Russo-Mongolian agreement and Protocol of the 21st of October, 3rd of November, 1912, respectively.[63] The agreement provides for the exclusion of Chinese influence in Mongolia. According to Article 1, Mongolia is " to admit neither the presence of Chinese troops on her territory nor the colonization of her land by Chinese." The main provisions of the protocol are as follows: Russian subjects shall enjoy the right to trade freely without payment of any duties, taxes or other dues and to open financial institutions and factories wherever they choose. Russian subjects shall be empowered to enter into agreements with the Mongolian

[61] See U. S. Consular Reports, No. 245, Oct. 20, 1913, page 354.
[62] See " Far Eastern Review," Vol. 10, page 290.
[63] The text of all Mongolian agreements, etc., is found in the *American Journal of International Law*, Vol. 10, No. 4, supplement, pages 239 ff.

Government respecting the working of minerals and timber, fisheries, etc. Russians shall retain the right to institute a postal service for the dispatch of letters and the transit of wares between all points of Mongolia and Russian consuls in case of need shall avail themselves of Mongolian Government postal establishments.

China had to acknowledge this state of affairs and in the Peking agreement of Nov. 5th, 1913, agreed not to deal with the Mongols without consent or assistance of the Russian Government, though she remains suzerain over Mongolia.

On Sept. 30th, 1914, Russia entered into another agreement with Mongolia which strengthened Russia's influence in that country as far as railways are concerned.[64] By this agreement Russia obtained the right to advise Outer Mongolia in deciding what railway lines to build and the method of procedure. Russia recognizes Mongolia's right to build the railways within its own boundaries if the funds can be raised there, but Mongolia is pledged to consult Russia before making concessions for railway construction to other nations. Since Mongolia is notoriously poor, it is evident that Russia has the exclusive right to build railways in this country.

The tripartite agreement of June 7th, 1915, is the final acknowledgment of the existing state of affairs.[65] Both

[64] See *Am. Jl. of Int. Law,* Vol. 10, No. 4, page 249.
[65] See *Am. Jl. of Int. Law,* Vol. 10, No. 4, page 251.

China and Russia agree to abstain from all interference with the internal administration of Outer Mongolia. Russian right to free trade is confirmed, while China is nominally acknowledged as suzerain. Practically, however, Outer Mongolia is under joint Russian and Chinese protection.

Mr. E. T. Williams sums up Russia's position in Mongolia: " These agreements, then, have considerably increased the political and commercial rights of Russia in Mongolia, and they thus tend to restore, if not to enhance, Russian prestige in the Far East which had been somewhat lessened by the result of the Russo-Japanese War." [66]

To the beneficent effects to be expected from Russia's position in Mongolia, Mr. M. D. Carruthers bears witness in his splendid work on " Unknown Mongolia." [67] " Taking for granted an autonomous Mongolia under the protection of Russia, we can prophesy far-reaching and fundamental changes in the lives of the people and in the future of the Mongol race. Mongolia will become — indeed, probably has already become — a land of activity and progress instead of, as formerly, a land of stagnation and suppression." And again: " The Russian influence has obviously an advantage over that of the Chinese. The Russians fraternize with the Mongol

[66] See *Am. Jl. of Int. Law,* Vol. 10, No. 4, page 808.
[67] See Carruthers, " Unknown Mongolia," pages 315, 317, and Introduction, page IV.

races, the race-barrier between them being much less marked than that between the Chinese and the Mongols." While Lord Curzon says in an introduction to the book: " We see. the Mongolian tribesmen, heirs of a mighty past, long withered under the blighting influence of degenerate Lamaism, but now turning to the risen sun of Russia to find a warmth and a protection which Chinese suzerainty has failed to give them."

These quotations lead us to a few concluding remarks about the secret of Russian success in Eastern Asia, based as it is on a national character and a disposition, different from the rest of Europe. We began our chapter by contrasting English and Russian governmental methods and shall now conclude with a few words about the differences in attitude. The attitude of Russia towards Asiatic peoples and the rule of her of subject races in Asia, may have been less humane, conscientious, and educative than the attitude of England and the rule by her of Asiatic subject races; but the Russians who exercise the administrative functions in the East are naturally more affable than the English, and are more indifferent to moral and religious propagandas. From origin, temperament, and personal habits, and through intimate contact with Asiatics from the dawn of history, the Russian is nearer to the Asiatic point of view than the Englishman. Says Wirt Gerrare: " Russia's . . . occupation of Northern and Central Asia has been of benefit to the inhabitants. It was only her methods of conquest which were unnecessarily severe. . . . Generally the Russian treatment of the native and subdued races if not perfect, or ethically correct, is not worse than that of other civilized Christian nations." [68] Vladimir maintains that " Russian annexation in Eastern Asia has been favorable to the Chinese people, opening new fields for their trading enterprise. The Russians have had the greatest toleration for the customs of the Chinese and for their local self-government, even when it was prejudiced to their legal sovereignty." [69] Even Lord Curzon in his book " Russia in Central Asia " admits that Russia has in her career of Asiatic conquest achieved a successful and a salutary end, and that Russia's dominion is " loyally accepted by the conquered races." [70]

Finally the relations between Russia and China cannot be understood without taking into account the fact that in spite of encroachments upon China by Russia, the two countries have never actually been in a state of war, excepting a few minor boundary disturbances. While European powers in general were not permitted to send diplomatic representatives to Peking until 1858, Russia had maintained a semi-official embassy there from 1692,[71]

[68] See Wirt Gerrare, op. cit., page 317.
[69] See Vladimir, op. cit., page 317.
[70] See Curzon, " Russia in Central Asia," Chapter X.
[71] See Ravenstein, " The Russians on the Amur," page 71.

and the expenses of the embassy even were partially sustained by China. The Russian representative has always been persona grata at the Court of China and has thus been able to enjoy a confidence denied to others.

Apparently nothing could shake Russia's faith in her Far Eastern policy. Russian policy in Asia has never changed; it may have been checked at times, but Russia quietly awaited her opportunity and at the right moment pressed forward and regained lost ground.

It is the absence of a definite or at least ulterior aim which distinguishes the Chinese policy of England from that of Russia; for in regard to Russia we have a clear and declared Asiatic policy, which during centuries has remained fixed.

No wonder then, that even in 1915, a Russian writer having in mind Manchuria and Mongolia, could write: " We find ourselves on the eve of new colonial adventures. In a word, the historical phase which was passed through before the Revolution, is about to be renewed." [72]

In brief, Russia's chances to reach her aims were greater than those of all other Powers and she would have been able to carry out her plans, if it had not been for two factors that were a curb to her expansion: Japan and the unrest within the Russian Empire.

[72] See Alexinsky, " Russia and the Great War," page 22.

CHAPTER IV

FRANCE

Of all Western countries, it has been the intercourse of France with China which, apart from trade, has been considerable. Both the earlier knowledge of the West acquired by China and that of China acquired by the West were mainly achieved by French missionaries, who also have played an important part politically. The accident of the dispatch of an envoy by the King of Annam to the court of Louis XIV turned the eyes of that monarch and of the ecclesiastics eastward to the possibility of obtaining political influence in Indo-China. In 1787 Bishop Pigneaux de Bretaine tried — though in vain — to bring Tonkin under French rule. His designs were frustrated by the French Revolution and only in 1858 another French force was dispatched to Indo-China. This time French attempts were successful, culminating in the final annexation of Cochin-China in 1862.

A protectorate over Cambodia was established in 1863. In the treaty of 1874, France acknowledged the independence of Annam; but Annam ceded — in Article V

119

— to France all territory already taken by France in the south.[1]

In 1884 the " Convention Fournier " was signed by which France bound herself to protect against all aggression by any nation whatever, and in all circumstances the southern frontiers of China and Tongking. This convention was confirmed by China in the treaty of 1885 under which France engaged herself to " re-establish and maintain order in those provinces of Annam which border upon the Chinese Empire." [2]   In Article VII China agreed that in case she should decide on constructing railways, she would have recourse to French industries.

This protectorate then formed the basis for further advance on China proper, the first and most important means of which was to be a railway into Yunnan.   And the first step towards a railway policy was marked by the convention of 1895, the fifth clause of which says: " It is understood that China, for the exploitation of its mines in the provinces of Yunnan, Kwangsi, and Kwangtung may call upon, in the first instance, French manufacturers and engineers, the exploitation remaining nevertheless subject to the rules proclaimed by the Imperial Government as regarding national industries.   It is agreed that railways either those already in existence

[1] See " British and Foreign State Papers," Vol. 65, page 375.
[2] See " Documents diplomatiques.   Affaires de Chine et du Tonkin, 1884–1885," page 283 ff.

or those projected in Annam may, after mutual agreement and under conditions to be defined, be continued on Chinese territory." [3]

On the strength of this agreement French railway enterprise in the south of China was seriously thought of and proposed to China in the years 1897 and 1898, when the construction of a comprehensive system of railways in Indo-China was mooted.

The growth of French influence and railway enterprise in Southern China marks the commencement of the realization of certain French ambitions for the furtherance of which Tongking was occupied. The most remarkable utterance in reference to France's policy is to be found in a most valuable work by M. Doumer, the late Governor-General of Indo-China, entitled, "L'Indo-Chine Française." He writes: "Le chemin de fer de pénétration au Yunnan, par la vallée du Fleuve Rouge, avait une importance politique qui n'était pas moindre que son importance commerciale indéniable. Longtemps, le Tonkin ne nous avait paru valoir que par l'accès qu'il donnait au Yunnan. On a très justement reconnu par la suite qu'il avait une valeur propre; mais

[3] See Rockhill, op. cit., No. 3.
The French text is to be found in "Documents diplomatiques, Chine, 1894–1898," pages 16–19, and reads: "La Chine pourra s'adresser à des ingénieurs et à des industries français pour l'exploitation des mines . . . les voies ferrées pourront être prolongées sur le territoire Chinois," etc.

ce n'était pas une raison pour oublier le but de notre pirse de possession." [4]

In other words, Tongking was occupied in order to provide a convenient means for the penetration of Southern China by a railway. But what were the motives for penetration? This question may in part be answered by going back to the motives behind the acquisition of the rest of French-China. They are thus summarized by Dubois et Ferrier in their work " Colonies Françaises." [5] " L'acquisition de la Cochinchine, le protectorat du Cambodge, sont dus, en effet, comme nos progrès en Afrique occidentale, à la ténacité des officiers. . . . Sans la guerre anglo-française de Chine qui, vite achevée, laissa disponibles des forces militaires en Extrême-Orient, nos amiraux n'auraient point sans doute obtenu les resources indispensables au succès. Au reste une politique essentiellement commerciale et dont l'espoir principal reposait sur la conquête de nouveaux marchés en pays peuplés devait tenir à prendre position à proximité de l'Empire Chinois. D'autres mobiles, en particulier le désir d'appuyer la propagande religieuse, renforcèrent cette première conviction. L'intelligence de nos d'escadre, le point d'honneur de ne pas lâcher prise, une fois engagés,

[4] See Doumer, " L'Indo-Chine Française," page 330. See also P. Leroy Beaulieu, " De la Colonisation," Vol. II, Chap. XI, Table de Matières, page 695: " Le but primitif de notre établissement an Tonkin: l'utilisation du ' fleuve Rouge ' pour la pénétration en Chine."

[5] See Dubois et Ferrier, " Colonies Françaises," pages 287 and 810.

firent le reste" . . . and again: "C'était aussi la
révélation de la richesse minière du Yun-nan, nouvel
attrait, et nouvelle raison pour les Français de s'intéresser
aux provinces septentrionales de l'empire d'Annam.
Occupation d'un pays plus salubre d'un débouché et d'une
voie d'accès de l'empire chinois, d'un fleuve plus maniable
que le Mékong, tels se présentaient aux esprits les avan-
tages d'une entreprise conseillée par Jean Dupuis et que
l'amiral Dupré espérait mener à bonne fin, grâce à l'ex-
périence particulière de Francis Garnier."

Mr. Hazen, the American historian, writes in his book
"Europe Since 1815": under the masterful influence of
Jules Ferry, prime minister in 1881, and again from
1883 to 1885, the Republic embarked upon an aggressive
foreign policy. She established a protectorate over
Tunis; sent an expedition to Tonkin, to Madagascar;
founded the French Congo. This policy aroused bitter
opposition from the beginning, and entailed large expenditures, but Ferry, regardless of growing opposition,
forced it through, in the end to his own undoing. His
motives in throwing France into these ventures were
various. One reason was economic. France was feeling the rivalry of Germany and Italy, and Ferry believed
that she must gain new markets as compensation for
those she was gradually losing. Again, France would
gain in prestige abroad, and in her own feeling of con-
tentment, if she turned her attention to empire building

and ceased to think morbidly of her losses in the German war. Her outlook would be broader. Moreover, she could not afford to be passive when other nations about her were reaching out for Africa and Asia. The era of imperialism had begun. France must participate in the movement or be left hopelessly behind in the rivalry of nations. Under Ferry's resolute leadership the policy of expansion was carried out, and the colonial possessions of France were greatly increased, but at the expense of political peace at home." [6]

France had to fall in line with the race for Empire and economic expansion. She was feeling the economic competition of all other nations. Furthermore France had retained her position as a great money-lending country; and she naturally preferred to invest her money in colonies and spheres of interest of her own.

Therefore, when in 1897, the era of spheres of interest, and the battle of concessions in China began, France lost no time in asserting herself. The greatest instrumentality of French ambitions in South China was M. Doumer. This energetic and ambitious statesman urged the adoption of a considerable railway program upon the French Government. In his speech to the Conseil Supérieur de l'Indo-Chine he referred to the aggressive attitude of other Powers, and emphasized the necessity of outbidding France's rivals in the South of

[6] See Hazen, "Europe Since 1815," page 353.

China. To use his own words: " La question des chemins de fer dans tout l'Extrême-Orient est aujourd'-hui à l'ordre du jour, comme en témoignent les efforts des rivaux de la France et les missions officielles envoyées en Chine. . . . L'Angleterre, avec une hardiesse que, de notre côté, nous n'avons pas montrée jusqu'ici, se met en marche par la Birmanie vers le Yunnan et le Ssetchouen qui semblaient réservés à notre pénétration commerciale. Pourtant, si nous savons vouloir, nous devons triompher dans cette lutte pacifique. Nous nous trouvons favorisés grâce aux facilités que nous donne la vallée du Fleuve Rouge pour atteindre le Yunnan. Mais il faut profiter de cette situation et joindre aux efforts faits par le Gouvernement de la Métropole l'action de la Colonie pour construire le réseau indochinois qui servira de base à notre pénétration en Chine." [7]

A similar view is expressed by Dubois et Ferrier: " L'intervention directe de plusieurs puissances européennes en Chine fait à nos hommes d'état un devoir pressant d'assurer cette nouvelle expansion de notre colonie, constituée d'hier, vers un pays libre de quatre cent millions d'habitants. . . . It faut donc pour rendre efficace le bienfait de ce voisinage, prendre l'initiative d'une pénétration qui nous rapproche le plus tôt possible des régions les mieux dotées. Aussi l'oeuvre de notre

[7] See Doumer, op. cit., page 326.

diplomatie commerciale des dix dernières années en Chine, est-elle une oeuvre profondément solidaire de notre expansion indo-chinoise." [8]

In 1897 and early in 1898, France used a policy of pressure upon China, similar to that exercised by other Powers. On April 10th the Chinese Government acquiesced in the following demands of France: [9]

1. The Chinese Government grants to the French Government, or to the French Company, which the latter may designate, the right to make a railway from the frontier of Tonking to Yunnanfu: the Chinese Government having no other responsibility but to furnish land for the road and its dependencies. The route of this line is actually surveyed, and will be fixed later on in agreement with the two Governments. Regulations will be jointly made.

2. The Chinese Government, in consideration of its friendship for France, leases the bay of Kuangchouwan, for 99 years, to the French Government, which may establish a naval station and coal depot there. The boundaries of the Concession will be fixed hereafter by agreement between the two Governments, after examination on the spot. The question of rental will be arranged later on.

[8] See Dubois, op. cit., page 824.
[9] See "Documents diplomatiques, Chine, 1894–1898," pages 49 to 51. English texts given by Rockhill, op. cit., Nos. 36 and 24. See also "British Blue Book, China," No. 1, 1899, Vol. CIX, No. 17.

3. When the Chinese Government organizes a definite Postal Service and places a high functionary at its head, it proposes to call for the help of foreign officers, and declares itself willing to take account of the recommendations of the French Government in respect to the selection of the staff.

4. With the purpose of assuring the relations of neighborliness and friendship between China and France; with the purpose, equally, of seeing the territorial integrity of the Chinese Empire maintained and, further, because of the necessity of taking care that no change be introduced in the existing situation as regards the provinces bordering on Tongking,[10] the Government of the Republic would attach particular value to receiving from the Chinese Government an assurance that it will not cede to any other Power all or a part of the territory of those provinces, either definitely or temporarily, or on lease, or by any title whatsoever.

A declaration concerning the non-alienation of the Island of Hainan had been given by the Chinese as early as March 15th, 1897.[11]

Having gained their points the French began railway construction. M. Doumer proposed to the Conseil Supérieur a comprehensive railway scheme for the

[10] The French text reads here: " Par suite de la nécessité né comté de veiller à ce que dans les provinces limitrophes du Tonkin, il ne soit apporté aucune modification àlétat de fait et de droit existant."
[11] See " Documents diplomatiques, Chine, 1894-1898," page 33.

French colonies, including a line from Haiphong to Hanoi with an extension to Yunnan. After the authorization of the scheme by this body M. Doumer proceeded to Paris to obtain the sanction of the French Chamber. The law authorizing the Government of Indo-China to borrow 200,000,000 francs for exclusive use of a railroad system was promulgated on the 25th of Dec., 1898.[12] In Article III the Government of Indo-China is authorized to grant a guarantee of interest to the Company which was to become the " concessionaire " of this line. The money which the colonial government might be called on to furnish is, in turn, guaranteed by the French Republic.

Owing to the Boxer troubles, little was done towards commencing railroad building in Yunnan and only the construction of the French colonial line from Haiphong to Hanoi and thence to Laokay was undertaken.[13]   But in 1901, M. Doumer succeeded in constituting a syndicate composed of the principal financial houses of Paris, and in concluding with this syndicate a convention for the building of the railway from Laokay to Yunnanhsien and for the working of the whole line from Haiphong to Yunnanhsien.[14]   The syndicate is the exclusive

[12] See Doumer, op. cit., page 329; and "Documents diplomatiques, Chine, Juin-Octobre, 1900."

[13] See Kent, op. cit., page 162.

[14] See Doumer, op, cit., pages 343 ff. and "Documents Diplomatiques."   See also Rockhill, op. cit., page 405.

concessionaire and is to build the railway from Laokay to Yunnan, with a total length of 468 kilometers at its own expense and risk, while it receives from the government of Indo-China, entirely constructed and ready for exploitation, the road from Haiphong to Laokay, being 385 kilometers long. The total line is conceded to the syndicate for 75 years, and is to be exploited at the expense and risk of the concessionaire with eventual share in the profits by the colonial government (avec partage éventuel des bénéfices entre celui-ci et le Gouvernement général).

The capital required for construction of the railway to Yunnan and for exploitation of the entire line from Haiphong to Yunnan was 101,000,000 francs and was constituted as follows: The stock capital of the syndicate, 12,500,000 francs; a subvention from the Government of Indo-China, another 12,500,000 francs; the rest, or 76,000,000 francs, in bonds guaranteed by the home government to the limit of an annuity of 3,000,000 francs yearly.

This convention was signed on the 15th of June, 1901, was presented three days later for ratification to the Chamber of Deputies by the Minister of the Colonies and the Minister of Finance, and was finally ratified by law of July 5, 1901. Immediately thereafter the " Companie française des chemins de fer de l'Indo-Chine et du Yunnan " was organized and the bonds issued.

On October 28th, 1903, the conditions under which
the extension was to be made on Chinese territory were
finally settled between the Chinese Government and the
French Minister.[15]   They comply with the concessions
granted to France on the 10th of April, 1898.   France
was to build, manage, and own the railway for eighty
years.   But " China retains full sovereign rights over
the line, which in the event of China's being at war will
not be considered neutral, but be placed under Chinese
orders.   China undertakes the sole responsibility of
policing and protecting the railway, and on no account
can the railway ask for the assistance of foreign troops."
There is to be no Chinese Government guarantee.   Indeed the Chinese have nothing whatsoever to do with
financing or managing of the line and they are deprived
of all control and profit.

In this latter respect French railway rights in China
are at variance with those enjoyed by Russia in Manchuria.   For Russia, as we have seen, had admitted the
Chinese to financial and even administrative participation — at least nominally.   But otherwise, there is little
distinction between French and Russian " control "; although French " control " is nominally exercised by a
private company and is therefore financial, the close
association of this Company with the French Government as manifested in the several conventions as well

[15] See Rockhill, op. cit., page 405.

as the motives behind French railway enterprise in Yunnan, leave no room for doubt that French control in
China, embodied in this French railway concession, is
in spirit, somewhat political. The railway policy of
France, like that of Russia, and as we shall see like that
of Japan, and to some extent that of Germany, "has
been a means to an end, an incident in a larger policy,
which can only be described as in intention a policy of
colonization." [16]

Nevertheless French policy in China proper has been
by no means as aggressive as that of Russia before the
Russo-Japanese War. With the exception of a few unsuccessful attempts at further concessions in the southern provinces, which were to be extensions of the existing
railway system, France did little in exploiting her sphere
politically.

Commercially, however, France took full advantage
of her privileged position: her "control" enabled her to
establish her trade at the expense of other nations by
means of preferential tariffs to the furtherance of French
commerce. No doubt the exceedingly high costs of construction and operation of the Yunnan railway forced
France to exact high charges. But these high charges
were not the only reason that prompted wealthy Chinese
citizens to contemplate a railway from Yunnan to Nanking which would break the French monopoly of the

[16] See Kent, op. cit., page 93.

carrying trade of Yunnan towards the sea. The best illustration of the unsatisfactory state of affairs is to be found in a consular report by Mr. G. E. Anderson, American Consul General at Hongkong.[17] According to this report the railroad to be constructed by Chinese is " to open Yunnan with the seaboard through Chinese territory and thus avoid present unfavorable conditions found in the transit tax charged for the transfer of foreign goods not of French or Indo-French origin crossing Indo-China and also to avoid the high freight rates over the French railway into Yunnan which now obtain." In another Report, Mr. Anderson remarks: " The restricted use and general unsatisfactory working of the railway is due to the abnormally and prohibitive high freight rates." [18]

The principal reason for such discrimination was, of course, to protect and advance the industries of France and her colonies. But it is interesting to note that in this France had no success. The British Minister to China, commenting on French railway enterprise in Yunnan, had remarked as early as 1898: " The impression in French railway circles is that a railway through Yunnan will not pay expenses." [19] And the railway did in fact not pay expenses for two reasons: Firstly, French trade in Southern China remained in-

[17] See U. S. Consular Reports, 1912, No. 233, page 1488.
[18] See U. S. Consular Reports, 1912, No. 27, page 503.
[19] See " China," No. 1, 1899, Vol. CIX, No. 459. Enclosure.

significant. Referring to the articles of the treaty of 1885 by which preference was to be given to French trade and industries, Mr. Douglas says: " The bulk of the trade of the country has, in the natural order of things, fallen into the hands of the Chinese, the British, and the Germans." [20] All preferential treatment of French goods has not increased French trade materially. Secondly: The exorbitant charges drove foreign trade away. To quote the *Far Eastern Review:* " As a natural consequence traders are again taking to the older and cheaper river and caravan routes." [21]

So much for French penetration of Yunnan. French ambitions were also reaching towards railway enterprise in Kwangsi, Kwangtung, and Szechuan. Especially Szechuan was earmarked for railroad exploitation. M. Doumer considered that the Laokai-Yunnanfu line would only demonstrate its true value when continued to Chengtu via Chungking. And the French Minister actually secured from China the right to construct the Yunnan-Szechuan railway for French interests.[22] Thus France gained for the loss of her share in the Pukow-Sinyang line. " At Chengtu she would link up with the ' Great achievement' of the Russo-Belgian combination, thus clasping hands across China with her ally on the north, and also would have the control of a large

[20] See Douglas, op. cit., page 387.
[21] See " Far Eastern Review," Vol 9, page 167.
[22] See " Far Eastern Review," Vol. 10, page 304.

section of the line eastwards to the Hupeh border as provided for in the Paris meetings of the Hukuang negotiations." [23]

Aside from this line various other railways were planned and partly conceded by China.[24] But only a few of these will stand a chance of eventual construction. The most important of the Franco-Russian-Belgian combination in which the French had a share of three-fifths of the capital, was the Peking-Hankow line.[25] We have seen that the terms of this concession were as favorable to the Chinese as the terms of the British concessions. They were purely financial.

The policy of France as far as the entire Far East is concerned was dominated by France's European policy which stood under the sign of the Russo-French Entente. The French nation is the great creditor of Russia and served as such, together with Belgium, as financial agent for Russian schemes in the Far East. The first joint financial enterprise was the Franco-Russian Government Chino-Japanese War Indemnity Loan of 400,000,000 francs, contracted in 1895. The money was almost exclusively subscribed in France. The first French railway loan contracted with Russian proclivities, as we have seen, was the Peking-Hankow line designed

[23] See *ibidem*.
[24] See Rockhill, op. cit., No. 59, " Kent Railway Enterprise in China," Chapter VXI.
[25] See " Far Eastern Review," Vol. 10, page 292.

to assist the achievement of the long cherished ambition of France to join hands across China with her great northern ally, Russia. Another Franco-Russian combination was the Shansi Railway Loan, contracted by the Russo-Chinese Bank and floated in France.[26] In 1903, the French and Belgians financed the Kaifenfu-Honan Railway, with L1,000,000, a supplementary loan of L640,000 having been floated in 1907. Both these latter railways and the French Taynan-Chengting line serve as feeders to the Peking-Hankow line. Another project of the Franco-Russian-Belgian combination is the Lung-Tsing-U-Hai line from Lanchow to Tungchow. The possibility of an early construction of most of the recent projects is very remote.

Finally French financiers participated with England, Germany, and America in the Four Power Negotiations, which will be a subject of investigation in Chapter VIII. France was to build the Kweichow-Chungking-Chengtu section as an extension to the so-called Hukuang system. According to the *Far Eastern Review:* "The financial arrangements will be equally shared by the four groups, but the French will benefit principally in the matter of construction as no share of the construction of the system provided for by the Hukuang Agreement was allotted to them." [27]

[26] See "Far Eastern Review," Vol. 10, page 294.
[27] See "Far Eastern Review," Vol. 9, page 305.

In concluding this chapter we want to remark that France, in attainment of her political ends, finds considerable aid through a close coöperation between her foreign finance and her foreign policy. Or, as Bland expresses it: "In France, where cosmopolitan finance has attained its highest form of organization, the Government has long since recognized the necessity for safeguarding the interests of French rentiers and at the same time for controlling capital as a source of national strength, by legislation which virtually prevents any French loan from going abroad without the full knowledge and approval of the French Government."[28]

In this direction France finds herself only surpassed by Germany and Japan, in which countries the coördination between political and financial activities is even closer and is not directed towards aiding the political designs of an ally but is employed to strictly national ends.

[28] See Bland, op. cit., page 287.

CHAPTER V

THE rise of Germany on the Chinese horizon is of quite recent date. Suggestions for the acquisition of a port on the Chinese seaboard had been made by German traders on various occasions, and political relations have existed between the two countries since 1861. Treaties were concluded in this year and in 1880. But nothing was accomplished in the direction of gaining a foothold in China until Kiaochau was occupied in 1897-98.

The occupation of Kiaochau had been decided upon in principle in 1896. Kent summarizes the events leading up to the occupation as follows: [1] " In that year — 1895 — it will be remembered, Li Hung Chang paid his celebrated visit to Moscow, being present at the coronation festivities of the present Tsar. On his return he passed through Germany. It was suspected at the time that Russia had secured valuable rights in North China and Manchuria. On being pressed Li Hung Chang steadfastly denied that this was so. Shortly after he had left the country, however, the German Government received

[1] See Kent, op. cit., page 140.

certain information that their suspicions had been correct. Thereupon Kiaochau, in anticipation of Russian aims, was mentally earmarked as a future territorial acquisition of Germany, who was badly in need of a naval station in Chinese waters, with the province of Shantung as their sphere of influence."

The opportunity to act upon this decision arrived in November, 1897, when two German missionaries were murdered in the province of Shantung. Immediately the incident became known, a German squadron anchored off the harbor of Kiaochau and landed troops, which occupied the town of that name. After a series of negotiations, Germany demanded and achieved the lease of Kiaochau for the purpose of a naval base, supposedly in compensation and guarantee for the crime. The cession found its expression in the convention of Peking on March 6, 1898:[2] "With the intention of meeting the legitimate desire of His Majesty, the German Emperor, that Germany, like other powers, should hold a place on the Chinese coast for the repair and equipment of her ships, for the storage of materials and provisions for the same, and for other arrangements connected herewith, His Majesty the Emperor of China cedes to Germany on lease, provisionally for ninety-nine years, both sides of the entrance of the Bay of Kiaochau."

[2] See Rockhill, op. cit., No. 8. See also Reichsanzeiger, April 29th, 1898.

It may be said that to Germany, perhaps, more than to any other country, the future of China at that period was indifferent. While ready to commit herself to the " Open Door " she also was prepared to benefit by the " Sphere of Interest " policy or a direct partition of China almost without preference as to which prevailed. The important thing to her was not the policy, but the benefit. If China attempted reconstruction, Germany was ready to lend her assistance. A strong China to her would be able to act as counterpoise to Russia, Great Britain, France and Japan. Should, however, the long threatened break-up of China become imminent, Tsingtau, the capital of Kiaochau, immediately became the kernel for a future German colony in the Far East. And Germany would have had her " place in the sun " in that part of the globe.

This policy of foresight and precaution was summarized by Baron von Bülow shortly after the cession of Kiaochau: " Es ist von der Aufteilung von China gesprochen worden. Eine solche Aufteilung würde jedenfalls nicht von uns ausgegangen sein; wir haben nur beizeiten dafür gesorgt, dass wir, was auch kommen möge, nicht ganz leer ausgehen. Wann sich ein Eisenbahnzug in Bewegung setzt hängt nicht immer von dem Belieben des Reisenden ab, wohl aber, dass er nicht den Anschluss versäumt. Den letzten beissen die Hunde. Wir wünschen aber nicht — und das möchte ich mit

besonderem Nachdruck betonen —, dass es zu einer
Aufteilung des Chinesischen Reiches komme. Ich
glaube auch heute noch dass es zu einer solchen Aufteilung in absehbarer Zeit nicht kommen wird. Jedenfalls
haben wir — und damit meine ich am besten sowohl die
Gründe, welche uns nach Kiaochau geführt haben, als
die Bedeutung von Kiaochau für uns zusammen-zufassen
— in Kiaochau eine strategische und politische Position
gewonnen, die uns einen bestimmenden Einfluss auf die
künftigen Geschicke Ostasiens sichert. Von diesem
festen Punkte aus konnen wir die weitere Entwicklung
der Dinge mit Ruhe und mit Gelassenheit abwarten.
Wir haben eine so grosse Aktionssphäre vor uns und so
bedeutsame Aufgaben, dass wir andere Mächte um die
ihnen gemachten Zugeständnisse nicht zu beneiden
brauchen. Die deutsche auswärtige Politik wird, wie
überall, so auch in Ostasien, ihren Weg ruhig, fest und
friedlich zu verfolgen wissen. Den Störenfried werden
wir nirgends spielen, das Aschenbrödel aber auch
nicht." [3]

[3] See Penzler, " Fürst Bülow's Reden," Berlin, 1907, page 30. An
English text is given in " China," No. 1, 1898, Vol. CV, No. 67, and
reads as follows: " Mention has been made of the partition of
China. Such a partition will not be brought about by us at any
rate. All we have done is to provide that, come what may, we ourselves shall not go empty-handed. The traveler cannot decide when
the train is to start, but he can make sure not to miss it when it
does start. The devil takes the hindmost. But we do not desire,
— and I beg to impress this point on you — we do not desire a partition of China, and I do not believe that there is an immediate
prospect of such a division. But in any case (and here, I think, I

The German demands following the occupation of Kiaochau naturally included a railway concession as one of the principal objects of the occupation. The lease of Kiaochau and a section of the hinterland, signed on the 6th of March, 1898, was followed by a railway convention of the same date under which the following provisions are made:[4] " I. The Chinese Government sanctions the construction by Germany of two lines of railway in Shantung. The first will run from Kiaochau and Tsinan-fu to the boundary of Shantung province via Weihsien, Tsinchow, Pashan, Tsechuen and Suiping. The second line will connect Kiaochau with Chinchow, whence an extension will be constructed to Tsinan through Laiwuhsien. The construction of this extension shall not be begun until the first part of the line, the main line, is completed, in order to give the Chinese an opportunity of connecting this line in the most advantageous manner with their own railway system. . . ."

" II. In order to carry out the above mentioned rail-

can best resume the advantages secured to us by the occupation of the port, as well as the reasons which induced it) ; in any case, I say, we have secured in Kiaochau a strategical and political position which assures us a decisive influence on the future of the Far East. From this strong position we can look with complacency on the development of affairs. We have such a large sphere of action and such important tasks before us that we have no occasion to grudge other nations the concessions made them. German diplomacy will pursue its path in the East as everywhere else — calmly, firmly, and peacefully. We will never play the part of mischief-maker, nor will we play that of Cinderella."

[4] See Rockhill, op. cit., No. 8.

way work a Chino-German Company shall be formed, with branches at whatever places may be necessary, and in this Company both German and Chinese subjects shall be at liberty to invest money, if they so choose, and appoint directors for the management of the undertaking." Article III provides among other things that " the object of constructing these lines is solely the development of commerce. In inaugurating a railway system in Shantung, Germany entertains no treacherous intention towards China, and undertakes not to unlawfully seize any land in the province." In conformity with the spirit of this provision: " The Chinese Government binds itself in all cases where foreign assistance, in persons, capital or material, may be needed for any purpose whatever within the Province of Shantung to offer the said work or supplying of materials, in the first instance to German manufacturers and merchants engaged in undertakings of the kind in question."

Following the acquisition of these rights Kiaochau was established as a commercial and strategic " point d'appui." The place was immediately declared open to foreign trade without distinction of nationality and an official report to the German Reichstag announced that no duties would be levied in the port of Kiaochau upon goods intended for consumption in German territory, excepting the excise duty on opium.[5]

[5] See Monthly summary of Commerce and Finance, U. S. Treasury Dept. Series, 1899–1900, Nos. 321, 323 b., Dec., 1899.

Furthermore in accordance with above mentioned convention the Chancellor of the Empire on the first of June, 1899, granted the concession for the construction and management of a railway from Tsingtau via Weihsien to Tsinan Fu, the provincial metropolis of Shantung, with a branch line to Poshan to a syndicate closely connected with the Deutsch Asiatische Bank and representing a wide circle of German industries and mercantile interests. This company was organized on the 14th of June, 1899, as The Shantung Railway Co., with headquarters in Berlin.[6] The capital was to be 54,000,000 marks.

The company was to be a German-Chinese Company. " Care is to be taken that Germans as well as Chinese may participate in the public subscription to the stock of the Company. More especially, shall subscriptions be opened in the suitable commercial centers of East Asia, and the amounts there subscribed shall receive proper consideration."

" The election of the President of the Board of Directors as well as the Chief Operating Official must be approved by the Imperial Government."

" German material shall be used, as far as possible, in the construction of the railways."

" The railway is to be equipped in due time with rolling stock according to the requirements of traffic. The

[6] See Rockhill, op. cit., No. 52.

material used shall be, as far as possible, of German origin."

Several articles provide for a control by the Governor of Kiaochau over the number of trains, fixing tariff and rates. Article VI authorizes the Imperial Government in case of such culpable action of the Company relative to one of the imposed obligations contained in the document, as should result in the railway's not being constructed or operated in due course, " to take over itself or cause to be taken over by a third party, the construction or extension of the railway and the organization or continuation of the traffic, all at the expense of the company."

Article X gives the Company the option until the end of 1908 to construct a railway from Tsinan to Ichow and from Tsingtau to Ichow, thus forming a triangle of railways covering all of the Province of Shantung. Article XI provides for a contribution from the yearly net profits of the railway to be applied to the expenditures of the Government of Kiaochau, which contribution is to be estimated as follows: " If after the opening of the traffic of the railway from Tsingtau to Tsinan, the net earnings of the railway would permit the payment of a yearly dividend of more than 5 per cent. of the paid-up capital which is used in operating the railway, there shall be paid into the Government-funds of Kiaochau the twentieth part of any surplus over 5 to 7 per cent., the tenth part of any surplus over 7 to 8 per cent. and so forth. . . ."

In Article XII " The Imperial Government reserves the right to purchase the railways to be constructed by the company in accordance with this concession after the end of sixty years, calculated from the date of the grant of the concession. The Imperial Government further reserves the right to buy at the end of every five years, including a one year's previous notice, all establishments, rolling stock, appurtenances, inclusive of the reserve and renewal funds earned by the railway enterprise, upon payment of twenty-five times the amount of the average dividends paid during the last five years from its earnings, or, at least, however, the commercial value of the actual existing railway plants, workshops and rolling stock."

The German railway line in Shantung, it may be finally remarked, is the only line of which China has not secured the right, some time or another, to assume the sole control.

In addition to or better, based upon these specific railway rights, Germany secured the dominating voice in the Province of Shantung with regard to employment of foreign capital, considering Shantung and adjacent territories as her " sphere of interest." The first step towards a recognition of the German sphere was the German participation in the Tientsin-Chinkiang, respectively — Pukow Railway following the German Minister's claim that the Shantung section of this line should be German.[7]   The German sphere of interest found confirmation by an arrangement between the British and German capitalists concerned.   It estimated the German sphere of interest to be: The peninsula of Shantung and the Hoangho Valley with connection to Tientsin and Chengting, or other point of the Peking-Hankow line, in the south with connection to the Yangtze at Chinkiang or Nanking.   The Hoangho Valley is understood to be subject to the connecting lines in Shansi forming part of the British sphere of interest, and to the connecting line to the Yangtze Valley, also belonging to the said sphere of interest.[8]

German control within the German sphere is based upon the railroad concession in Shantung.   At first sight, the principal control provisions quoted above show a similarity of German control to that exercised by France and Russia.   The concession was granted to the German Government, which, in turn, designated leading German financial interests, united in the Deutsch-Asiatische Bank, to form a railroad company for the actual construction of railways within the sphere.   Since this Company is a private concern, the control provisions are nominally financial.   But the final supervision over traffic, tariff, and rates as well as the share in profits by

7 See above, page 45.   8 See above, page 46.

the Government of Kiaochau, and the provision, that the line, under certain conditions, may or shall be taken over by the Imperial Government shows that German control is also political. Indeed, as Prince Bülow has suggested in his speech, the railroads extending from Kiaochau could be considered the first step towards German colonization in China, in case other Powers should set the example. Nevertheless German control differs in so far from Russian control, as Germany has taken no direct steps towards establishing a political influence such as was contemplated by Russia in Manchuria previous to the Russo-Japanese War. Neither has Germany, by rates or any other means, discriminated against the free enjoyment of the treaty rights of other nationals within her sphere.

Germany considered Shantung as a field for commercial exploitation — much as England considered her sphere in the Yangtze in the light of its economic possibilities. Both Powers, though alive to a possible partition of China, had the political independence and territorial integrity of China in mind. German and English policy found its expression in a mutual Agreement, concluded during the Boxer troubles, namely on Oct. 16th, 1900. The agreement reads: [9]

1. " It is a matter of joint and permanent international interest that the ports on the rivers and littoral of China

[9] See Rockhill, op. cit., No. 14.

should remain free and open to trade and to every other legitimate form of economic activity for the nationals of all countries without distinction; and the two Governments agree on their part to uphold the same for all Chinese territory as far as they can exercise influence.

2. "Her Britannic Majesty's Government and the Imperial German Government will not, on their part, make use of the present complication to obtain for themselves any territorial advantages in Chinese dominions, and will direct their policy towards maintaining undiminished the territorial condition of the Chinese Empire.

3. "In case of another Power making use of the complications in China in order to obtain under any form whatever such territorial advantages, the two contracting Parties reserve to themselves to come to a preliminary understanding as to the eventual steps to be taken for the protection of their own interests in China."

To Germany Kiaochau was the economic key to Shantung and Shantung the economic key to northern China. On the completion of the Tsingtau-Tsinanfu Railway Germany endeavored to derive the full pecuniary advantages of her monopoly. To quote the *Far Eastern Review:* "When Tientsin is closed by ice during the winter months the export trade of North China is paralyzed, with the exception of the small volume which finds its way out of the harbor of Chinwangtao. A

glance at the map will show that much of the trade now
enjoyed by Tientsin, could be diverted to Tsingtao with
considerable advantage to a vast section of North China,
and consequent profit to Germany. The construction of
any line or lines connecting the Northern or German
Section of the Tientsin-Pukow with the Peking-Hankow
Railway, would create a revolution in the old established
channels of trade, and instead of flowing northwards to
Peking and then down again to Tientsin the products of
Southern Chihli, Shansi, Shensi and Honan would follow the shortest and most direct route to the sea, over
the German lines to Tsingtao." German diplomacy has
been keenly alive to this fact, and the German Minister
has on several occasions approached the Chinese Government to secure a concession to construct a line to connect Chengtingfu with Techow and Kaifeng with Yen-
chow. According to Mr. P. C. Kent, in his valuable
book on " Railway Enterprise in China ": " the German
Minister has only succeeded in arriving at an understanding with the Chinese Government to the effect that
in the event of the Chinese Government deciding upon
the construction of these lines and requiring the assistance of foreign capital, German capitalists will be
allowed the first refusal of the Concession. A glance at
the map is sufficient to indicate the commercial importance of these railways to Shantung and Tsingtao. . . .
With the thoroughness characterizing her foreign trade

policy, Germany has carefully protected and insured her position in Shantung, and as the construction of these lines will ultimately become imperative for the development of China, she may well afford to bide her time with the calm assurance that her plans will mature. Her position is further safeguarded by the terms of the Tientsin-Pukow Loan Agreement, Clause 19 of which reads: Branch lines in connection with the railway line mentioned in this Agreement may be built by the Imperial Chinese Government with funds at their disposal from Chinese sources, if thought advisable, and if foreign capital is required preference will be given the Syndicate." [10]

In 1913 Germany made another step forward. On December 31st of that year, a preliminary agreement was signed between China and Germany for the construction of two new railways in Shantung province, one from Kaomi, west of Tsingtau, to Ichowfu and Hanchuang, on the railway line connecting Pukow with Tientsin, and the other from Tsinanfu to some point on the Peking-Hankow Railway. In the final agreement the line from Kaomi was to run to Hsuchowfu and to form a junction with the Tientsin-Pukow Railroad. "Under the Kiaochow Convention of March 6, 1898, China conceded Germany the right to build railways in Shantung under German Company laws, and

[10] See "Far Eastern Review," Vol. 9, page 156.

while the railroad from the port of Tsingtau to Tsinanfu
was so constructed, Germany decided not to follow the
same practice in the future, agreeing to forego the
privileges in that direction and permitting China to build
the lines upon conditions similar to those under which
other railroads have been constructed.[11] These new
lines then were to be Chinese-state-owned, but German
capital and materials were to be employed in their construction and the Chief Engineer and the General
Manager were to be German subjects." A construction
of these lines in the near future is of course very un-
likely.

The comparatively large and speedy successes of German finance in China were, last not least, due to the
forward methods of the German bankers. German
finance and industry are more highly organized and
coördinated to the specific purpose of extending national
interests abroad than is the case with any other power
in the world. And at the same time German diplomacy,
in coöperation with German industry and finance, is
striving to extend and promote the trade secured by the
foresight of German business men. "Not only does
the German Foreign Office keep in touch with the movements of its financiers abroad . . . but it has
come to pass, as part of a regularly organized system,

[11] See "Far Eastern Review," Vol. 11, page 18. See also Vol. 10
Dec., 1913.

that all the great financial industries are directly associated with groups of manufacturers and industrialists,
so that the whole force of politics, industries and finance
moves forward, along predetermined lines, to a common
goal." [12]   This goal is the extension of markets for German goods and the purpose of German foreign investment within such markets is to help home enterprise.

That the participation of German banks in industrial
enterprises and in capital investments abroad has to be
concentrated upon exclusively German success is maintained by all the foremost German authorities on finance.
Riesser says: [13] " Internationale Geschäftsbeziehungen
und internationale Emissionen dürfen immer nur Mittel
zur Erreichung nationaler Ziele sein und müssen sich in
den Dienst der nationalen Arbeit stellen."   And in Waltershausen's book " Kapitalsanlagen im Ausland " we
find the following passages: [14] " Für die Zukunft der
deutschen Volkswirtschaft ist es von Wichtigkeit, dass
der Kapitalsexport planmässig im nationalen Sinn ge-
leitet wird. . . ."   " Die Auslandsbanken, obwohl Er-
werbsinstitute, übernehmen mit ihrer Tätigkeit national-
wirtschaftliche Funktionen zugunsten des Waren und
Kapitalsexports."   And in order to illustrate that a

[12] See Bland, op. cit., page 287. See also Withers, op. cit., page
109.
[13] See J. Riesser, " Die deutschen Grossbanken," page 293.
[14] See Sartorius von Waltershausen, " Kapitalsanlagen im Ausland," page 293.

monarchical form of Government like the German is, according to German opinion, best fitted for carrying out a broad national foreign policy we quote a passage from Treitschke:[15] "Der König kann sehr viel genauer beurteilen, wie es in der Welt draussen wirklich steht, als der einzelne Untertan oder auch eine republicanische Parteiregierung. Eine weit in die Zukunft rechnende Politik wird nur dem möglich sein, der wirklich in Zentrum steht."

It was then to the specific purpose of preserving and expanding markets for German industry that a number of leading financial institutes as early as 1889 founded the Deutsch-Asiatische Bank, which we have mentioned before. The formation of a group or syndicate for Asiatic business in 1890 was the natural consequence of the establishment of the bank.[16] The purpose of the syndicate was to be concerted underwriting of state and provincial and railway loans in China, Japan and Korea and the establishment of railroad and mining companies. The spirit that animated the syndicate may be illustrated by a further quotation of Riesser: "Die Ubernahme von Anleihen für China wurde ein Kampfobject zwischen allen den Staaten, die da wussten, dass in erster Linie der financielle Einfluss dem politischen die Wege bahnt."

One of the first greater successes of the syndicate

---

[15] See Treitschke, "Politik," II, page 55.
[16] See Riesser, op. cit., page 403.

represented by the Deutsch-Asiatische Bank was the coöperation with the British Hongkong and Shanghai Bank in contracting one-half of the Chino-Japanese War indemnity loan of 1896 and 1898.[17] The two banks furthermore coöperated in 1905 in the Exchange Adjustment of the Boxer Indemnity (being L1,000,000), in 1908 and 1909, in contracting the Imperial Chinese Government Tientsin-Pukow Railway Loan totaling L5,000,-000 of which the Deutsch-Asiatische Bank issued L13,150,000 — and finally in 1910 in the Tientsin-Pukow Railway Supplementary Loan of L4,800,000.[18] The participation of the Syndicate in international loan negotiations will be dealt with in the respective chapter.

Though the means of Germany deviate materially from Anglo-Saxon means and therefore have even before the war provoked misunderstandings, there is nevertheless to be found a frequent financial coöperation between the two countries. Even as late as the spring of 1914, English-German coöperation in certain railway enterprises was found desirable. The latest German attempt to connect the Tientsin-Pukow Railway with the Peking-Hankow Railway was made by a German industrial organization apparently independent of the Deutsch-Asiatische Bank. Referring to this organization the *Far Eastern Review* remarks: " The scheme is doubtless intended to comprise all the most important German

[17] See Chapter VIII.   [18] See Chapter VII.

industrial concerns, and there is some reason to suppose that it is desired to secure English coöperation. The theory that Germany and England are now natural partners in Chinese business is being systematically propagated." [19]

British-German coöperation, however, has been shattered through the present war. The elimination of Germany's interests and " control " in China and the appearance of Japan as the — at least for the time being — arbiter of Eastern Asia has changed the whole aspect of the Far Eastern question.

[19] See " Far Eastern Review," Vol. XI, page 98.

CHAPTER VI

JAPAN

THE advance of Russia into Eastern Asia had for many years given rise to anxiety on the part of Japan, whose island home lies so close to the shores of the neighboring continent that the possession of the Asiatic coast line by a strong Western Power would, it was recognized, be a standing menace to the independence of the Empire. "In 1873 the Iwakura embassy had returned from Europe deeply impressed by the power and activity of the Western world, and especially by the aggressive designs of Russia. A memorandum drawn up by Okubo Toshimichi declared that Russia, always pressing southwards, is the chief peril for Japan. It is not surprising, then, that the safeguarding of Japanese interests in Korea became the first aim of Japanese policy." [1] Japan's very safety demanded that neither of her great neighbors, Russia and China, should obtain an undue share of influence in the Far East. It was therefore with some alarm that in 1891 Japan learned that the Tsar's government had determined to construct a line

[1] See Douglas, op. cit., pages 191, 192.

156

of railway through Siberia to connect European Russia
with Vladivostok. As a first countermove, Japan, upon
realizing the designs of Russian policy and the weakness
of the Chinese Government, sought to establish Korea
as an independent state, the latter then being under
Chinese suzerainty. But while it was in Japan's interest
to strengthen and reform Korea, it was to China's interest to keep the Korean government corrupt and weak
and to withstand Japanese aspirations.

The opening of the Korean question, then, marked
the beginning of a new era of Chino-Japanese relations. In this period there are three great events which
may serve as landmarks, namely the Chino-Japanese War
of 1894-95, the Russo-Japanese War of 1904-05, and
Japan's participation in the present world war.

Early in 1894, a rebellion broke out in Korea, Japanese troops occupied Seoul, Korea renounced Chinese
suzerainty, all of which finally resulted in the Chino-
Japanese War, at the very beginning of which Japan
concluded a treaty of alliance with Korea against China.[2]
This war may be said to be a direct outcome of Japan's
resolution to reconstruct Eastern politics on a modern
basis and of China's persistence in the old methods. Its
result was a clear evidence of the superiority of the
modern methods which Japan had adopted.

The effects of the war upon the situation in the Orient

[2] See Rockhill, op. cit., page 429.

were far-reaching. Japan's rise as a modern nation in
the estimate of the world may be said to date from this
time, especially since the same year saw a treaty of commerce and navigation between England and Japan, which
serves as the Magna Charta of Japan in regard to her
dealings with foreign states.

The conclusion of peace by the treaty of Shimonoseki
on the 17th of April, 1895,[3] was received with universal
enthusiasm throughout Japan. It was realized that this
treaty, coming after the trimphant victories which had
everywhere distinguished Japanese arms, must place the
country in the front rank of nations; and the extension
of territory awarded by the cession of the Liaotung peninsula and Formosa served to flatter the pride of the
people. But when, a week later, the joint protest against
the occupation of the Liaotung peninsula, or any other
portion of the mainland of China, made by Russia,
France and Germany, reached Japan, the people evinced
the utmost indignation. It was realized, however, that
it would be hopeless to enter on a contest with three
first-class Powers, and, after a moment's hesitation, the
government decided to renounce the Liaotung peninsula,
and demand an additional indemnity of seven and a half
million pounds sterling in its place. These terms were
agreed to by China.

The lesson was not lost on the Japanese; the humilia-

[3] See Rockhill, op. cit., page 14.

tion to which they had been subjected, left an indelible
impression upon their minds; and they at once determined so to strengthen their position as to enable them
to hold their own on all future occasions. They set on
foot an elaborate scheme of naval and military expansion which it was hoped would yield the expected results
within a few years.

If the enforced surrender of the Liaotung peninsula
left in the minds of the Japanese a burning sense of
wrong, subsequent events forced upon them the conviction that, sooner or later, Japan would have to enter on
a life-and-death struggle with the Muscovite power.
Further machinations of Russia in Korea led Japan to
come to agreements and to make arrangements relative
to the independence of Korea and neutral rights.[4]   Of
still greater importance was the circumstance that the
absorption of Manchuria by Russia had begun.   The
greatest event in this direction — and of far reaching
consequences — was the taking of Port Arthur; the
manner in which Russia obtained possession has been
already described.

The news of the lease produced a wild excitement in
Japan. Not only had Russia ousted Japan by the force
of specious pleas, but in direct conflict with those pleas
she had taken possession of one of the most hardly-won
prizes of the late war. The nation was stirred to its

[4] See Rockhill, op. cit., Nos. 67, 68, 69.

depths; and it was only by the wise and weighty pressure which was brought to bear by the Elder Statesmen and the Government that war was averted. Here again Japan showed a great self-control. Her only answer to Europe's aggression on Chinese territories — of the " battle of concessions " — was a demand on China that the province of Fuh-kien opposite Formosa shall not be alienated to any other government.[5]

In the troublous times to follow Japan had further occasion to show growing strength, vigor and thoroughness. This was especially the case during the Boxer movement, the immediate consequence of which was to see Japan's position in regard to China vastly improved. The most important thing that contributed to this state of affairs was the admirable behavior of the Japanese troops during the occupation of Peking, by which Japan also gained Europe's admiration.

To enumerate further successes of Japan in Korea against Russian aspirations and to go into detail as to the immediate causes of the then impending war is here of little interest. The main point is that from the day on which Japan was forced to forego the cession of the Liaotung peninsula as part of the hard-won spoils of the China war, she had steadfastly kept in view the prospect of one day having to fight Russia for her national existence. In the nine years which had elapsed

[5] See Rockhill, op. cit., No. 26.

between the last incident of the Chinese War she had
made every preparation that human foresight and energy
could ensure to fit herself for the conflict which her
statesmen felt to be inevitable. Consequently the war
was a success.

Before treating the most important and far reaching
consequences of the war and the events following it,
events which are of particular interest to our investigation, we have to understand the motives and forces which
have been at the root of the foreign policy of Japan
and all the great changes which have taken place. At
the outset we cannot doubt that the intense feeling of
patriotism among the Japanese and the determination
to make their country stand in a position of equality
with foreign nations were the most important factors
in the movement which has profoundly changed all the
conditions of Japan. The great national mission of
Japan is, according to Count Okuma,[6] " to harmonize
Eastern and Western civilizations in order to help bring
about the unification of the world, to effect a right harmony between its own and the outside civilization."
The main ideas with which the Japanese started when
they decided to adopt Western methods were embodied
in the principles proclaimed on oath by the late Emperor
on the occasion of his accession to the throne on March
14, 1868, the principal passage of which reads as fol-

[6] Naoichi Masaoka, " Japan's Message to America."

lows:[7] " All purposeless precedents and useless customs being discarded, justice and righteousness shall be the guide of all actions. . . . Knowledge and learning shall be sought after throughout the whole world, in order that the status of the Empire of Japan may be raised ever higher and higher."

Behind the patriotic motives there are strong economic and political forces which have influenced the foreign policy of Japan. The rapid increase in population and the necessity for outlets not only for the surplus population but also for the surplus industrial products, has been forcing Japanese statesmen to consider the problems involved, and like the statesmen of other countries they have sought them in the settlement of numbers of their people in foreign countries and in an extension of their foreign markets. The development of industry in Japan is making the country directly dependent on the produce of other countries for the food of its population and on raw materials.

Japan's difficulties were increased through the financial situation. Baron Yamamoto, minister of finance, several years ago warned the nation as follows:[8] " As we are all aware, this country bears a heavy burden of foreign loans and has to pay yearly a large amount of money both in principal and interest. To relieve this

[7] Henry Dyer, " Dai Nippon," page 27.
[8] Whelpley, " The Trade of the World," page 243.

situation, means to be resorted to must be those of the development of export trade, while it is equally important to check the growth of all that tends to increase the outflow of specie and to make efforts to lighten the burden of national debt."

The whole industrial situation in Japan up to late years was critical. Whelpley remarks: [9] " The dissemination of Western ideas and the increasing cost of living are bringing about a state of restlessness and dissatisfaction potent with serious possibilities. Industrial unrest, strengthened by the increasing spirit of individual freedom may ultimately prove a serious check to the pace which now marks the progress of Japanese foreign trade. Increased wages, shorter hours of labor and even the most elementary protection of women and children now working in factories will threaten the present advantage of the Japanese in the cost of production."

Reasons such as enumerated make it clear that Japan found it difficult to compete with European and American goods and all of the circumstances referred to force Japan to look towards the mainland of Eastern Asia as the principal outlet of her goods and surplus population, and as the source of raw materials. The most desirable outlets from a geographical position, sparse-peopled territory and undeveloped resources are Korea and Manchuria, a part of Mongolia, and probably Eastern Siberia,

[9] Whelpley, op. cit., page 253 ff.

while China proper offers the multitude of people as a basis for a wide market.

All of the circumstances mentioned above furthermore may be said to be responsible for the tendency of Japan in the earlier years of her occupation to monopolize such parts of Manchuria as she held in control. They also are responsible for the methods employed by Japan, in those regions, and for the measures taken.

Of great significance in this connection is a statement of Baron Makino, Minister of Agriculture and Commerce: [10] " China has people, and population is what makes trade. No other country in the world offers so vast a field for trade. With the growth of education and the development of material progress possibilities of commercial enterprise in China are simply unlimited. The anxiety of the powers to enter into more and more intimate trade and political relations with China cannot but excite intense interest in Japan; for China is our nearest neighbor, our best customer; and our commercial and political relations with that country are superior to those of any other nation. . . . It is true that Japan enjoys a profitable trade with many countries of the West; . . . but this occidental trade at its best is difficult to handle with any satisfactory degree of achievement; for it is always more difficult to deal with highly developed commercial nations than with those less ad-

[10] See Whelpley, op. cit., page 247 ff.

vanced in modern progress. Trade with peoples of lower social standards is always more easy and profitable. . . . To-day the mind of Japan is all toward China as the commercial hope of our future, not to say anything of our geographical and racial advantages with that country. It is our ambition to be to the East what Great Britain is to the West. . . . It is not too much to say that a great part of our hope for future financial rehabilitation in Japan depends upon how we can further develop trade with China."

It is now our purpose to investigate measures taken and methods used by the Japanese in their relations with China in accordance with the task set in the introduction.

The terms of the Treaty of Portsmouth in 1905 gave an inadequate result to Japan for all her costly sacrifices. Japan had to take the entire financial burden on her own shoulders, not being able to force Russia to pay her an indemnity. But on the other hand, Russia ceded to Japan her leasehold rights in the peninsula of Liaotung including the fortress of Port Arthur and in Article VI, the ownership of the southern section of the Manchurian Railway, from Port Arthur to Kwangchengtze, and all its branches, " together with all rights, privileges, and properties appertaining thereto in that region, as well as all coal mines in the said region, belonging to or worked for the benefit of the railway." [11]

[11] " British and Foreign State Papers," Vol. 98, page 735.

In Article VII " Japan and Russia engage to exploit their respective railways in Manchuria exclusively for commercial and industrial purposes and in no wise for strategic purposes."

The arrangement was subject to the consent of the Imperial Chinese Government, which was promptly forthcoming in a convention of Dec. 22, 1905.[12] In Article I the Imperial Chinese Government consents to the transfers and assignment made by Russia to Japan, while in Article II " The Imperial Japanese Government engages that in regard to the leased territory as well as in the matter of railway construction and exploitation, they will, so far as circumstances permit, conform to the original agreements concluded between China and Russia."   In Article VI, " The Imperial Chinese Government agrees that Japan has the right to maintain and work the military railway line constructed between Antung and Mukden and to improve the said line so as to make it fit for the conveyance of commercial and industrial goods of all nations."

With the transfer to Japan of Russia's railway interests in South Manchuria, the policy of acquiring influence by economic means was adopted by Japan as the last of the Powers and was practiced with great skill. The exploitation of South Manchuria was not undertaken by the Japanese Government directly but

[12] " British and Foreign State Papers," Vol. 98, page 740.

by a powerful joint-stock company in which the Government is the largest shareholder. On June 1, 1906, the South Manchurian Railway Company was promulgated for the purpose of operating the railway between Dalny and Changchun, including branch lines, the line between Antung and Mukden, and the rich coal mines of Fushun an Yentai.[13]

The "authorized capital" of the concern was Yen 200,000,000, of which the Government held Yen 100,000,000. Of the rest only Yen 20,000,000 were subscribed by and issued to the public.[14] The Government shares represent the value of the lines as agreed upon when the company took them over, together with the Yentai and Fushun collieries. The railroad is actually run by the proceeds of L12,000,000, of debentures issued in London and mostly held by British investors. These debentures are guaranteed, both as to capital and interest, by the Japanese Government. The Japanese Government also guaranteed the shareholders six per cent. on the capital, while the Company pledged itself to repay the Government as soon as the railway should begin to yield sufficient revenue.

The South Manchurian Railway Company was formally established on Nov. 13, 1906, with Baron S. Goto

[13] For the status of the South Manchurian Railway, see Harrison, op. cit., pages 258 ff. See also "Far Eastern Review," Vol. 11, pages 385 ff.
[14] See "China Year Book, 1914," Chapter on Communications.

as President, and the railways and mines were taken over
by this company from the Japanese Government in the
spring of 1907. The new company engages largely in
enterprises other than those of a public carrier. The
scope of the new undertaking indeed was large: The
company runs a regular service of ships between Dairen
and Shanghai, and owns the fleet of the Dairen Steamship Company, coasting in the Gulf of Pechili. The
Fushun Colliery, about twenty-five miles east of Mukden, as well as coal fields and mines at various other
places, are under its control. It constructed the great
harbor works at Dairen and owns the wharves and
shipping facilities of Port Arthur. It provides electric
current for many towns and gas as well, where required.
It has large hotels at all these places. The Japanese
furthermore encouraged industries and brought new
ones. They have settled in the country by large numbers, and to-day it is estimated that there are 100,000
Japanese in South Manchuria. They, last not least, keep
an army in the country, the so-called " railroad guards."
For in a supplementary agreement to the Portsmouth
Treaty " The High Contracting Parties reserve to themselves the right to maintain guards to protect their respective railway lines in Manchuria. The number of
such guards shall not exceed fifteen per kilometer, and
within that maximum number the Commanders of the
Japanese and Russian armies shall, by common accord,

fix the number of such guards to be employed, as small as possible, having in view the actual requirements." [15]

Full advantage of this clause has been taken by both parties and in the absence of accurate figures the length of line controlled may be taken as the measure of the local military strength. The 700 miles of the South Manchurian Railway system together with other substantial concessions aggregating to over one thousand miles enable Japan to keep a formidable army in the country.

Apart from the system itself, the Company owns from 46,000 to 50,000 acres of land, capable of very profitable cultivation, the so-called "zones." [16] About these zones Harrison remarks: [17] "On receiving from the Russians the expropriated lands within the railway zone, with numerous buildings, the Japanese set aside a certain proportion for the needs of the railway, and transferred the remainder to the settlement administrations to be made use of." According to Harrison "the settlement chief, or socho, superintends the lands and buildings of his division, looks after scholastic, medical, and sanitary matters, and is responsible for proper precautions against accidents from fire or other cause. He is also responsible for the preparation of the annual estimates and accounts of revenue and expenditure. To

[15] See "British and Foreign State Papers," Vol. 98, page 739.
[16] See Lawton, "Empires of the Far East," Vol. II, pages 1166 ff.
[17] See Harrison, op. cit., page 256. See whole Chapter XIV of Harrison.

this official also belong the imposition of taxes, supervision of the development of trade and industry in his division, and inspection of public property. . . . All the orders and arrangements of the socho must be submitted to the Chief Director of the railway, by whom they must be sanctioned."

In addition to this and as an additional precaution against hasty legislation there exist special committees in several places, subordinate to the Chief of the settlement, " but nevertheless at liberty to complain to the Chief Director of the railway against what, in their opinion, constitutes illegal action on the part of the above official." " The subjects of every nationality are free to settle in the railway zone, but they must conform to all the rules and regulations of the railway company, and must also pay a specific tax for public purposes." In the zones the railway builds schools, maintains hospitals, provides for medical and technical college training, creates townships, erects public buildings, makes roads, constructs telegraph lines and installs telephones.

In short, this great and most efficient concern exercises not only commercial privileges but also administrative functions. The company runs the whole railway system, including all lands connected with it, for the Japanese Government; the South Manchurian Railway Company is merely another name for the Japanese Gov-

ernment. The Japanese Government owns four-fifths
of the paid-up capital; the bonds are guaranteed by the
Government; and the railway is under supervision of
the Japanese Railway Board, which controls all the
nationalized railways of Japan.[18] And through the
" guards," the company works hand in hand with the
military authorities. While Chinese sovereignty is
respected within the concession, the railway with all its
lands constitutes an imperium in imperio. Not only do
the Japanese enjoy immunity from taxation by the
Chinese authorities but the preservation of law and
order in the concession is intrusted to the railway company, and the Japanese Government enjoys a correspond-
ingly large influence within the whole of the Japanese
Sphere of Interest, i.e., all of South Manchuria.

Japanese control in South Manchuria, then, as based
upon the railway concession inherited from Russia, is
much similar to that exercised by Russia in all Manchuria previous to the Russo-Japanese War, although
the South Manchurian Railway Company is much more
of a commercial enterprise than the Chinese Eastern Railway.

In order to firmly establish Japanese commerce on
a definite basis Millard informs us [19] that " the Government called some prominent financiers and merchants

[18] See Harrison, op. cit., page 279.
[19] See Millard, op cit., page 206.

into consultation, and a somewhat extraordinary program was advanced. For purpose of directing, under the Government, an energetic campaign to monopolize the foreign trade of Manchuria, what is known as the Manchurian Export Guild was formed in 1906. It included most of the greater commercial guilds in Japan, such as the Osaka Boseki, Mige Boseki, Kanakin Seishoku, Tenima Ormono, and the Okayama Boseki. It was announced that Mitsui and Company were to act as general agents for the guilds and the Government, through its branches in Manchuria; and the Yokohama Specie Bank, the Government's fiscal agent in Manchuria, was to lend its coöperation." Foreign traders thus were confronted by the competition of the Japanese merchants, financiers and Government combined. A great aid to Japan's trade was, as the *Far Eastern Review* remarks, "the economic paternalism of the Japanese Government, which takes the shape of subsidies to steamship lines and the provision of cheap capital to merchants. Assistance is also freely given to the Japanese firms by the Japanese semi-official bank in Manchuria." [20]

In the matter of railways, Japan also took advantage of the post-bellum situation in order to secure substantial advantages for herself or at least to obstruct designs of outsiders, contrary to her interests. A significant

[20] See " Far Eastern Review," Vol. 11, page 488.

and interesting case is offered by the Hsinmintung-Fakumen project. In November, 1907, the Chinese Government made a contract with the British firm of Pauling and Co. for the construction of an extension of the Imperial Railways of Northern China from the northern terminus Hsinmintung to Fakumen,[21] fifty miles in length. When the matter became known at Tokyo, Japan objected to further extension of this line on the ground that it would injure the South Manchurian Railway. The *Far Eastern Review* remarks to this: " The Peking Agreement of Dec. 22, 1905, entered into between China and Japan contained a secret clause which bound China not to construct prior to the recovery of the South Manchurian Railway any main line in the neighborhood of and parallel to that railway or any branch line which might be prejudicial to its interests. This self-denying claim, in which China in effect surrendered her sovereign rights to construct railways in Manchuria, was made public and successfully invoked by the Japanese Government to obstruct and cause the abandonment of the projected Fakumen Railroad, a branch line of the Northern Railways from Hsinmintung to the market town of Fakumen. China had entered into a signed agreement with a British financial corporation to supply the funds and contracted with a British construction firm to build the line. China's undoubted

[21] See " Far Eastern Review," Vol. 11, page 383.

intention was to test the strength of the secret agreement referred to, and if Japan acknowledged her right to build the Fakumen extensions, the line was to be carried on northwards towards Changchun." [22]   The final triumph of Japanese diplomacy found its expression in Article I of the Sino-Japanese Agreement of Sept. 4, 1909, referring to Manchuria: "The Government of China engages that in the event of its undertaking to construct a railway between Hsimintun and Fakumen, it shall arrange previously with the Government of Japan." [23]

The British-American project from Chinchow to Aigun met with a similar fate owing to joint Russo-Japanese representations.   Other objects of Japanese policy were the Hsinmintung-Mukden and Antung Mukden railroads.[24]   During the war Japan had constructed a narrow gauge railway between Hsinmintung and Mukden.   This line was transferred to China in 1908.   The Japanese, however, knew how to retain control over the line.   The Antung Mukden railroad likewise was constructed during the war by the Japanese army for military purposes, and Japan insisted after the war, that she be permitted to reconstruct and operate the line as a branch of the South Manchurian Railway.   The respective clause VI in the Sino-Japanese Peking Treaty reads

[22] " Far Eastern Review," Vol. 9, page 153.
[23] See " British and Foreign State Papers," Vol. 102, page 393.
[24] See " Far Eastern Review," Vol. 11, page 383.

as follows: " The Imperial Chinese Government agrees that Japan has the right to maintain and work the military railway line constructed between Antung and Mukden and to improve that said line so as to make it fit for the conveyance of commercial and industrial goods of all nations." [25]

Finally, Japan secured the Kirin-Changchun Railway and extensions from China. Section b, Clause 3, of the Convention between Japan and China signed at Peking April 15th, 1907, provides as follows: " If the Kirin-Changchun line should hereafter build branch lines or an extension the construction of such lines shall rest of right with the Chinese Government, but if there shall be a lack of capital, application should be made to the South Manchurian Railway Company for an arrangement." [26] The branch lines as well as a participation in the construction of the Changchun-Kirin line were conceded to Japan in the above mentioned agreement of Sept., 1909.

Referring to several of the later railway concessions the *Far Eastern Review* remarks: " By securing from China the control and administration of the Kirin-Changchun Railway, and extension of the agreements governing the South Manchurian and Antung-Mukden railways, as well as the refusal of foreign loans for

[25] See " British and Foreign State Papers," Vol. 98, page 740.
[26] See " British and Foreign State Papers," Vol. 101, page 275.

railway purposes in South Manchuria, Japan has the satisfaction of knowing that she is now dominant in the country so far as railways are concerned even if she is eventually unable to extract from China the consent necessary to establish her overtly in a supremely favored position politically." [27]

All the railways in Southern Manchuria, constructed or projected, belong to the one great Japanese state-controlled system, and have connection with the Korean military system. They consequently will, aside from commercial advantages, afford Japan further facilities for the movement of troops in case of necessity. This is the opinion of Harrison, who writes: " It can scarcely be doubted that, in the event of hostilities with Russia or China, Japan would not be long about availing herself of the Chinese railroads, which would render her position even stronger." [28]

In this connection it has to be remembered that South Manchuria stands simultaneously with the supervision of the railway company under the military régime of Japan, based upon an addition to Article III of the Treaty of Portsmouth which grants the right to Japan to maintain " guards " to protect the railway lines in Manchuria.

[27] See " Far Eastern Review," Vol. II, page 375.
[28] See Harrison, op. cit., page 292.

For the first two years after the war, the military grip of Japan upon Manchuria was a tight one and not without legal basis. Japan and Russia in Article III of the Portsmouth treaty mutually engaged: [29]

1. " To evacuate completely and simultaneously Manchuria except the territory affected by the lease of the Liaotung Peninsula, in conformity with the provisions of additional Article I annexed to this treaty "; and

2. " To restore entirely and completely to the exclusive administration of China all portions of Manchuria now in the occupation or under the control of the Japanese or Russian troops with the exception of the territory above mentioned."

The war then was followed by a " legal " evacuation period during which Manchuria was under Russian and Japanese military control. The end of the so-called evacuation period however, was set as late as March, 1907, thus giving Japan and Russia the right to a two years' military administration of the country. It was mainly during this period that many accusations by Western journalists were heard, pointing to breaches of the doctrines of the " open door," " equal opportunity " and " integrity of China " on the part of Japan. But inasmuch as it is the purpose of this treatise to investigate and analyze well-founded facts, we cannot pay any

[29] See " British and Foreign State Papers," Vol. 98, page 735.

attention to alleged breaches of obligations. Besides, Japan has at several occasions acknowledged and bound herself to adherence to the principles in question.

First of all Japan had answered favorably to Mr. Hay's "Open Door Policy" circular sent to the Great Powers in 1899.[30] On January 30, 1902, the Anglo-Japanese Offensive and Defensive Alliance was concluded,[31] which clearly sets forth that the two governments are specially interested in maintaining the "independence and territorial integrity of the Empire of China and the Empire of Korea, which pledge has been broken since by Japan, and in securing equal opportunity in those countries for the commerce and industry of all nations."

The same words recur in the agreement between Japan and Great Britain of August 12, 1905, made public September 27, 1905 — being a renewal of the alliance — which in its preamble gives the preservation of the integrity of China and maintenance of equal opportunity for all as one of its principal objects.[32] The alliance was reaffirmed in 1911.

In Article IV of the Portsmouth Treaty "Japan and Russia reciprocally engage not to obstruct any general measures common to all countries which China may take

[30] The text of the circular, etc., will be dealt with in its proper place in the following chapter on the United States.
[31] See Rockhill, op. cit., No. 16.
[32] "British and Foreign State Papers," Vol. 98, page 136.

for the development of the commerce and industry of Manchuria." [33]

In 1907 two understandings were arrived at by Japan as one party, reaffirming the adherence to the principles in question. Namely: On June 10, 1907, an agreement was concluded between Japan and France, in which the following words occur: " The Governments of Japan and France, being agreed to respect the independence and integrity of China, as well as the principle of equal treatment in that country for the commerce and sub-jects or citizens of all nations," etc.[34]

And on July 30th of the same year, a convention between Japan and Russia took place in which the two parties " recognize the independence and territorial integ-rity of the Empire of China, and the principle of equal opportunity in whatever concerns the commerce and in-dustry of all nations in that Empire." [35]

On November 30, 1908, a more explicit understanding than that of 1899 was reached between Japan and the United States. At that date notes were exchanged between the two countries, declaring their policy in the Far East as follows: [36]

Article II: The policy of both Governments unin-fluenced by any aggressive tendencies, is directed to the

[33] " British and Foreign State Papers," Vol. 98, page 735.
[34] See " British and Foreign State Papers," Vol. 100, page 913.
[35] See " British and Foreign State Papers," Vol. 101, page 462.
[36] See *American Journal of International Law*, January, 1909.

maintenance of the existing status quo in the region mentioned (Pacific Ocean) and to the defense of the principle of equal opportunity for commerce and industry in China.

Article IV: They are also determined to preserve the common interests of all powers in China by supporting by all pacific means at their disposal the independence and integrity of China and the principle of equal opportunity for the commerce and industry of all nations in that Empire.

And finally two years later Japan and Russia, in the convention of July 4th, 1910, in relation to Manchuria declared in Article II:[37] " Each of the High Contracting Parties undertakes to maintain and respect the status quo in Manchuria resulting from all the treaties, conventions, and other arrangements concluded up to this date either between Russia and Japan or between those two powers and China."

The different conventions, agreements and so forth, clearly prove that Japan is committed as deeply as other powers are, to the policy of the " open door," " equal opportunity " and " integrity of China."

It has always been Japan's emphatic contention that so far no measure she has taken is inconsistent with the doctrines to which she has pledged herself. Indeed strict adherence to the principles of international law

[37] See " British and Foreign State Papers," Vol. 103, page 586.

has according to Count Okuma always been considered the wisest diplomacy. Count Okuma says: " I desire here to emphasize the fact that foreign intercourse must above all things be planned on a large scale, for all diplomatic projects have immediate interest for the whole world; and that, since foreign policy, or rather, national policy, must be fixed, unchanged, and continuous, the best method of diplomacy is to adhere strictly to all principles of international law." [38]

In further defense of Japan against any accusations we have to consider that Japan could not afford to be altogether altruistic in her methods as long as Russia's policy in the north remained a menace to Japan. Concerning Japan's justification of her actions in Manchuria by reference to Russian precedent we only need to refer to our chapter on Russia. There we find that the Manchurian Railway, which according to Article VI of the Portsmouth Treaty was transferred to Japan " together with all rights, privileges and properties appertaining thereto " and which according to Article VII was in no wise to be exploited for strategic purposes, had enabled Russia to dominate the whole of Manchuria and at once had given her a predominance in North China which placed other Powers at a marked disadvantage. Russia's railways in that region were specific means for encroach-

[38] See A. Stead, " Japan by the Japanese," chapter Foreign Policy by Count Okuma, page 221.

ment upon China, that is, for Russian imperialistic expansion. The Russification of the country had proceeded at a fast pace and other Powers — as for instance Great Britain — were effectively excluded from railway participation. So also was China, and, although according to the original agreement the Chinese Eastern Railway was to be under Chinese direction, only Russians managed the lines.

Is it not surprising, then, that Japan, when she followed Russia in the possession of the railroads and in the control of the country, was determined to reap the fruits of her hard won victories without restriction and that Japan, however altruistic her professions might have been, would not readily subordinate her own interests to those of China or other foreign powers. For, on behalf of Japan it has been urged that any special advantages she has secured in Manchuria are merely in the nature of reward for her vast expenditure in blood and treasure, and that, moreover, the control over Manchuria and other parts of Eastern Asia that might follow — together with the exploitation of those regions — is a matter of life and death for her welfare and national existence, especially in the face of international economic competition.

In this connection it is not only curious but also very significant to observe that Russia in the North followed — or at least pretended to follow — Japan's policy in the South. Behind the attitude of both was the ever present envy and mistrust of the other. Both have been enemies and might have continued to be had it not been for the Russian revolution. Therefore we have been given books bearing titles such as the " Coming Struggle in Eastern Asia."

The impartial observer, then, must not permit himself to be deceived by the apparent amity between the two Powers which was established in 1907.

The Russo-Japanese business agreements in relation to Manchuria concluded on July 30th, 1907, and on July 4th, 1910 — being of the most friendly nature — lead to the assumption that Japan and Russia had made up their minds for matter of convenience — and for the time being — to divide their interests in Manchuria between them, to strengthen their positions in their respective " spheres " and to guarantee to each other the status quo against any possible intruder: for such had supposedly appeared in the person of Mr. Knox, who had urged internationalisation of certain railways in Manchuria and construction of new lines under international auspices.[39] The efforts of the American state department only hastened the conclusion of the second agreement which took place on the Fourth of July.

We quote the text in full: [40]

[39] See Chapters VII and VIII.
[40] See " British Foreign and State Papers," Vol. 103, page 586.

1. With the object of facilitating communications and developing the commerce of the nations, the two high contracting parties agree to extend to one another their friendly coöperation with a view to the improvement of their respective railway lines in Manchuria, and the perfecting of the connecting services of the said lines, and to abstain from all competition prejudicial to the realization of this object.

2. Each of the high contracting parties undertakes to maintain and respect the status quo in Manchuria resulting from all the treaties, conventions, and other arrangements concluded up to this date, either between Russia and Japan or between those two Powers and China. Copies of the said arrangements have been exchanged between Russia and Japan.

3. In the event of anything arising of a nature to threaten the status quo mentioned above, the two high contracting parties shall enter each time into communication with each other with a view to coming to an understanding as to the measures they may think it necessary to take for the maintenance of the said status quo.

The agreement having been happily concluded, Japan endeavored to take full advantage of the special position she held in South Manchuria. William Blane, in an article, " The Japanese in China," [41] writes in 1915:

[41] See *Journal of the American Asiatic Association* of July, 1915, page 175.

" When I went over the works of the South Manchurian Railway Company two years ago I was struck by the permanent nature of everything that had been done and that was in progress . . . extensive additions and costly improvements were in progress at the great harbor of Dairen, and the main line track was being doubled throughout. The Company was making huge profits and sinking the greater part of them in constructional works which will serve for a century after the present agreements expire. The *Engineer* of the 13th of November, 1914, after describing the railways and drawing attention to the brief tenure of the company adds: In the face of these things Japan, instead of preparing to reap returns, keeps putting more money into the business every year."

This Russo-Japanese agreement of 1910 then was the crowning achievement of Japan's Manchurian policy. What are the principal reasons for Japan's success? In the pursuance of her foreign policy it was primarily the monarchical-military and at the same time somewhat oligarchical-paternalistic form of her government — partly traditional, partly copied from Germany — which being well adapted to the special means of Japan has made her so successful. That diplomacy has to rest with the crown and the crown's advisers, and that the goal, once set must not be changed, has been early recognized by Japanese statesmen. Says Count Okuma: " The kind of diplomacy that changes with its director is most pernicious and dangerous." [42]   And Douglas, commenting upon the Proclamation of the Japanese Constitution, says: " Foreseeing that, in order to maintain national independence and to fulfill what they regard as their mission in the East, unity of control and the unfettered power of employing all the forces of the nation would be indispensable conditions of success, they resolved, while enlisting the sympathies of the people, to secure the crown against excessive popular interference." [43]   Among other means by which Japan has attained her predominant position in Asia is to be placed first in historic importance the alliance of Japan with Great Britain.   The immediate practical benefit of the alliance to Japan, renewed during the Russo-Japanese War and again in July, 1911, was the readier sale of Japanese bonds.   The surplus from war funds borrowed in England enabled the Japanese Government to invest in the South Manchurian Railway.   Debentures floated in England have resulted in the expansion of that great corporation at the expense of others, last not least, of Great Britain herself.   While Britain, France, Belgium, Germany, and even Russia to some extent have financed their railways themselves, Japan alone has constructed and equipped her railways on

[42] See Count Okuma in A. Stead, " Japan by the Japanese," page 222.

[43] See Douglas, op. cit., page 201.

the mainland of Asia almost exclusively with foreign capital, and that capital — thanks to the alliance — is British.

But above all, the alliance permitted Japan's entry into the present World War. When Japan took possession of the territory originally leased to Germany, she did so as the representative of Great Britain and her European Allies. At that time Count Okuma claimed that:[44] "Every sense of loyalty and honor obliges Japan to coöperate with Great Britain to clear from these waters the enemies who in the past, the present and the future menace her interests, her trade, her shipping, and her people's lives." And the Japanese Foreign Office addresses the United States as follows:[45] "Aside from the history of the seizure of the place by Germany and her conduct dating back to and including her intervention, in conjunction with Russia and France after the Chino-Japanese War, it is absolutely necessary to eliminate such possession completely if Japan is to restore immediately complete peace in the Far East in accordance with the terms of the Anglo-Japanese alliance."

Japan's interference, then, is based upon Article A, of the Preamble in conjunction with Article I, of the treaty

[44] *Journal of the American Asiatic Association,* Vol. XIV, No. 8, page 231.
[45] *Ibidem.*

of July 13, 1911, the Preamble stating as object of the treaty,[46] "the consolidation and maintenance of the general peace in the regions of Eastern Asia and India."

The seizure of Kiaochau was connected with various substantial advantages to Japan:

Japan occupied the Kiaochau-Tsinanfu Railway. This seizure apparently meant a violation of Chinese territory and the Chinese protested against it as falling entirely out of the German territory which has been leased. But from the Japanese standpoint it would be dangerous to leave the railway in the hands of the enemies.

Furthermore, the Japanese secured from China substantial and exclusive concessions in Shantung. To that end the two countries concluded a treaty respecting the Province of Shantung and exchanged notes respecting the restoration of the leased territory of Kiaochau Bay — both on the 25th day of the 5th month of the 4th year of Taisho.[47]

We quote the important passages of the treaty, etc.: Article I: The Chinese Government agrees to give full assent to all matters upon which the Japanese Government may hereafter agree with the German Government relating to the disposition of all rights, interests and concessions which Germany, by virtue of treaties or other-

[46] See " British and Foreign State Papers," Vol. 104, page 173.
[47] The text of the treaties and exchange of notes is to be found in the Supplement to *American Journal of International Law*, Vol. 10, No. 1, pages 1 ff.

wise, possesses in relation to the Province of Shantung.

Article II: The Chinese Government agrees that as regards the railway to be built by China herself from Chefoo or Lungkow to connect with the Kiaochau-Tsinanfu railway, if Germany abandons the privilege of financing the Chefoo-Weihsien line, China will approach Japanese capitalists to negotiate for a loan.

And as to Kiaochau: " When after the termination of the present war, the leased territory of Kiaochau bay is completely left to the free disposal of Japan, the Japanese Government will restore the said territory to China under the following conditions:

" 1. The whole of Kiaochau bay to be opened as a commercial Port.

" 2. A concession under the exclusive jurisdiction of Japan to be established at a place designated by the Japanese Government."

Finally, on the same day Japan and China concluded a treaty and exchanged various notes respecting South Manchuria and Eastern Inner Mongolia. The respective agreements of this date may be summed up as follows: [48] The lease of Port Arthur and Dalny and the terms of the South Manchuria Railway and the Antung-Mukden Railway shall be extended to 99 years.

[48] See *American Journal of International Law,* Vol. 10, No. 1, Supplement pages 5 ff.

Japanese subjects in South Manchuria and Eastern Inner Mongolia receive further privileges as to trading, traveling and leasing properties.

China will open suitable places in these regions as commercial ports.

Railroad agreements between Japan and China may be revised as soon as more advantageous terms than those existing are granted to other foreigners.

Japanese subjects shall investigate and select mines in specified areas within said regions.

Loans for building railways in said regions may be negotiated with Japanese capitalists in preference to other foreigners.

If foreign advisers or instructors on political, financial, military or police matters are to be employed in South Manchuria, Japanese may be employed first.

Finally, China and Japan agreed upon coöperation in the working of the Hanyehping Company, China not being permitted to convert it into a state enterprise nor to cause it to borrow and use foreign capital other than Japanese.

These agreements require but little commentary. They strengthen Japan's position in Southern Manchuria through the extension of all leases to 99 years and through the provision of foreign advisers, if such are to be employed, they give to Japan more exclusive concessions and privileges in Shantung, Eastern Inner

Mongolia and Southern Manchuria; and they give preference to Japanese financiers in the building of new railroads in said regions.

There are three points we now mean to emphasize:
Firstly, the United States-Japan agreement of November
2, 1917, has dispersed much of the doubt and suspicions
about Japan's ulterior aims in China which had been
voiced so freely throughout the world.[49] Referring to
Japan's special interests in China the agreement says:
" The United States has every confidence in the repeated
assurances of the Imperial Japanese Government that,
while geographical position gives Japan much special
interests, they have no desire to discriminate against the
trade of other nations or to disregard the commercial
rights heretofore granted by China in treaties with other
powers."   The agreement also denies that the two governments " have any purpose to infringe in any way
the independence or territorial integrity of China."
Secondly, Japan's control over her new spheres will again
primarily be exercised through railways; in other words,
it will be financial.   Thirdly, Japan is extending her
control in China while the control of other nations is
declining.

Japan has taken over the protection of British interests
in Eastern Asia. She has eliminated Germany. She
has concluded a treaty with Russia, which came near

[49] See especially F. McCormick, " The Menace of Japan."

to being an alliance. The text of this treaty, concluded on July 3rd, 1916, reads as follows:[50]

" The Imperial Governments of Japan and Russia, having resolved by united efforts to maintain permanent peace in the Far East, have agreed upon the following.

" Article I: Japan will not become party to any arrangement or political combination directed against Russia. Russia will not become party to any arrangement or political combination directed against Japan.

" Article II: In case the territorial rights or special interests in the Far East of one of the contracting parties recognized by the other contracting party are menaced, Japan and Russia will act in concert on the measures to be taken in view of the support or coöperation necessary for the protection and defense of these rights and interests."

Mr. Kawakami makes the following comment upon this treaty: " To call the new convention an alliance is, perhaps, not quite correct. A treaty of alliance must provide mutual obligations on the part of the high contracting parties to render armed assistance to each other in case their respective interests are in danger. The most significant part of the convention lies in the wide application which it apparently permits. While it is obvious that the covenant aims chiefly to secure the respective interests of the contracting parties in Man-

[50] See *American Journal of International Law,* Suppl. X, 239.

churia and Mongolia, its scope is not restricted to these two countries but covers the entire Far East." [51]

An additional agreement between Russia and Japan throws considerable light upon the real value of the convention to Japan.[52] The Chinese Eastern Railway has been sold by Russia to Japan from Changchun to Laoshaokou for six million yen. The length is 71 miles. Russia furthermore has extended to Japan the privilege of navigating the Second Sungari River. In other words Japan's interests in Manchuria are expanding. Russia was under considerable obligation to Japan for war supplies, and otherwise; the convention was the quid pro quo.

Last not least has Japan welcomed the decision of the United States to enter the war. She has gladly offered the protection of American interests on the whole Pacific and a close coöperation with the United States in the pursuance of the war. In return for these services she has now received an acknowledgment of her " special interests " in China by the government of the United States. Aside from the declarations of adherence to the " open door " and " independence and territorial integrity of China " principles, the agreement of November 2, 1917, contains the following most important passage: " The governments of the United States and

[51] See K. K. Kawakami, *Review of Reviews,* Sept., 1916.
[52] See Kawakami, *ibidem,* and " Far Eastern Review," Aug., 1916.

Japan recognize that territorial propinquity creates special relations between countries, and, consequently, the government of the United States recognizes that Japan has special interests in China, particularly in the part to which her possessions are contiguous." This agreement is doubtless one of the greatest achievements of Japanese diplomacy. It removes all danger of friction between the United States and Japan; it secures the independence and territorial integrity of China and the " open door " and equal opportunity for commerce and industry in China; it opposes " the acquisition by any government of any special rights or privileges that would affect the independence or territorial integrity of China or that would deny to the subjects or citizens of any country the free enjoyment of equal opportunity in the commerce and industry of China "; and last, not least, it recognizes Japan's predominant position in Eastern Asia.

Thus is Western control in China gradually declining while Japanese control is in the ascendancy. All treaties, conventions, agreements, and alliances through which Japan is consolidating her position are concluded for the consolidation and maintenance of a permanent peace in Eastern Asia. This is by no means merely a phrase. It is the crux, the key, to the whole Far Eastern Question: A Permanent Peace, but a Japanese Peace, a Pax Japonica. Such is the secret, then, of Japan's control in China: an Eastern Asiatic Doctrine with Japanese Hegemony — Japan to be Sovereign Arbiter and High Protector of Eastern Asia. To quote the words of Aubert: " Paix Japonaise de l'Extrême-Orient, comme jadis il y eut une Pax Romana dans le monde méditerranéen, comme aujourd'hui il y a une paix Britannique aux Indes, une paix Américaine dans les deux Amériques, c'est-à-dire la paix dans une partie du monde imposée par un peuple fort qui ne tolère point de querelles privées ou d'agression étrangère sur le territoire qu'il protégé. Arbiter souverain entre les peuples Extrême-Orientaux et leur défenseur contre toute attaque des puissances occidentales, tel peut apparaître le Japon." [53]

[53] Aubert, " Paix Japonaise," page 37.

CHAPTER VII

THE United States is the only great nation that has maintained throughout its relations with China a consistent attitude of unselfishness and of a decent consideration and respect for the sovereign rights of the Chinese people. Not only has the United States done this in her own relations, but she has frequently attempted to make others do likewise, be it indirectly through her example or directly through soliciting adherence to the open door principle. It is obvious then that without a reference to America's policy our investigation would be incomplete — although the United States has herself never exercised any " control " whatsoever.

From the inception of American relations with China at the birth of the republic, when George Washington commissioned as consul Major Shaw, down to the present day America has made no attempt to obtain an acre of Chinese territory. She has contented herself with the development of an extensive trade and diplomatically with the establishment and maintenance of friendly relations. Thus the American Secretary of State declined in 1857 to Lord Napier to participate in the

Chinese War.[1] In the instructions to the American representative in China of May 30th, 1859, we find the following significant passage:[2] " This country, you will constantly bear in mind, is not at war with the Government of China, nor does it seek to enter that empire for any other purposes than those of lawful commerce, and for the protection of the lives and property of its citizens. The whole nature and policy of our Government must necessarily confine our action within these limits, and deprive us of all motives, either of territorial aggrandizement or the acquisition of political power in that distant region." In the following year the United States concluded a Treaty of Peace, Amity, and Commerce with China. In this treaty, made at a time when the Chinese Government appeared to be peculiarly friendless, we find the remarkable stipulation that " if any other nation should act unjustly or oppressively (towards China) the United States will exert its good offices, on being informed of the case, to bring about an amicable arrangement of the question, thus showing their friendly feelings."[3]

It was the American envoy to China, Anson Burlingame, who first advocated the " open door " and called a halt to the attempts at selfish exploitation which appeared to guide the foreign powers in their attitude

[1] See Senate Document 35th Congress, 1st Session, Vol. 12, No. 47.
[2] See Senate Document 35th Congress, 1st Session, Vol. 12, No. 47.
[3] See Malloy, " Treaties," Vol. 1, page 212, Article I.

toward China. So well had he gained the sympathy and friendship of the Chinese people that he was invited to become the head of a Chinese embassy to all the treaty powers. The Burlingame treaty, negotiated between China and the United States, was strikingly fair and gave full recognition to China of her rights of eminent domain over all her territory, even including that occupied by foreign merchants.[4] In Article VIII "The United States, always disclaiming and discouraging all practices of unnecessary dictation and intervention by one nation in the affairs or domestic administration of another, do hereby freely disclaim and disavow any intention or right to intervene in the domestic administration of China in regard to the construction of railroads, telegraphs or other material internal improvements."

The formal declaration of the open door doctrine was made in 1899. Towards the close of the nineteenth century the commercial and political position of the United States in China had begun markedly to decline. The reason for this is mainly to be found in the activities of other Powers. "When in 1894,— remarks Rockhill[5] — the new era of rapid encroachment on China by its powerful neighbors began, it became apparent to the United States that if it did not take measures to check the movement its trade would be wiped out, its

[4] See Malloy, "Treaties," Vol. I, page 236, Article I.
[5] See *Journal of the American Asiatic Association,* Vol. XIV, No. 11.

religious and educational interests restricted, and its influence and prestige with the Chinese reduced to naught." The Washington Government readily recognized the danger and initiated international action in China's favor. With a view to securing equal opportunities in the development of China's trade, which was believed to offer vast fields for commercial and financial enterprise, America's first object was to prevent the partition of China, and particularly the absorption of Manchuria by Russia, and also the acquisition by any single Power of exclusive interests and " rights." To that end Mr. Hay sent his famous notes to the several Powers. The so-called policy of " open door," for the first time officially pronounced at that occasion, demanded formal assurances that each power within its respective sphere of whatever influence:[6] " First: Will in no way interfere with any treaty port or any vested interest within any so-called ' sphere of interest ' or leased territory it may have in China.

" Second: That the Chinese treaty tariff of the time being shall apply to all merchandise landed or shipped to all such ports as are within said ' sphere of interest ' (unless they be ' free ports '), no matter to what nationality it may belong, and that duties so leviable shall be collected by the Chinese Government.

[6] See Rockhill, op. cit., No. 28. See also " Foreign Relations of the United States," 1899, pages 128 ff.

" Third: That it will levy no higher harbor dues on vessels of another nationality frequenting any port in such ' sphere ' than shall be levied on vessels of its own nationality, and no higher railroad charges over lines built, controlled or operated within its ' sphere ' on merchandise belonging to citizens or subjects of other nationalities transported through such ' sphere ' than shall be levied on similar merchandise belonging to its own nationals transported over equal distances."

All powers promptly acknowledged adherence to the principle of the " open door " as set out in the circular. But the proposition, as Mr. Willard Straight remarks, " favorably received at first and reaffirmed in the negotiations which followed the relief of Peking, won the adherence of other nations not because of any particular consideration for China but because of their mutual jealousy and their realization that partition would impose upon them responsibilities which they might find it difficult to bear.   They did not therefore surrender the ports which they had forcibly leased, but their acceptance of the ' open door ' doctrine nevertheless marked the beginning of a financial and commercial, rather than territorial, definition of their respective interests." [7]

The United States should find several other occasions to reënforce the demand for " open door."   The next step taken in China's favor was a circular note of July

[7] See W. Straight, " China's Loan Negotiations," page 124.

3, 1900, inviting the Powers coöperating in China against the Boxers to adhere to the principles maintained by the United States on the Chinese question.[8]   In this circular Mr. Hay declared the policy of the United States to be: " To seek a solution which may bring about permanent safety and peace to China, preserve Chinese territorial and administrative entity, protect all rights guaranteed to friendly powers by treaty and international law, and safeguard to the world the principle of equal and impartial trade with all parts of the Chinese Empire." In 1901 the United States refused to assent to the imposition of an oppressive indemnity upon China which would make her the fiscal vassal of foreign powers for an indefinite period. Later on the American Government remitted to China a substantial proportion of its Boxer indemnity. On February 1st, 1902, Mr. Hay sent a memorandum to the Powers protesting against monopolistic concessions made to Russia by China, which would " distinctly contravene treaties of China with foreign Powers, affect rights of citizens of the United States by restricting rightful trade, and tend to impair sovereign rights of China and diminish her ability to meet international obligations." [9]

America's adherence to the " open door " doctrine found finally an expression in the agreement between the

[8] " Foreign Relations of the United States," Appendix to 1901, Affairs in China, page 12.
[9] See " Foreign Relations," 1902, page 275.

United States and Japan of November 30th, 1908,[10] in which we find the following passages: " The policy of both Governments, uninfluenced by any aggressive tendencies, is directed to the maintenance of the existing status quo in the region above mentioned and to the defense of the principle of equal opportunity for commerce and industry in China. . . . They are also determined to preserve the common interest of all powers in China by supporting by all pacific means at their disposal the independence and integrity of China and the principle of equal opportunity for commerce and industry of all nations in that Empire." The year 1908 saw also an unofficial reaffirmation of the same policy, when Mr. William Howard Taft addressed the Chamber of Commerce at Shanghai. Since the foreign policy of the United States was subsequently to be directed by Mr. Taft, the respective passage of his speech requires quotation:

" The United States and others who sincerely favor the open door policy will, if they are wise, not only welcome, but will encourage this great Chinese Empire to take long steps in administrative and governmental reform, in the development of her natural resources and the improvement of the welfare of her people. In this way she will add great strength to her position as a self-respecting Government, may resist all

[10] See Malloy, " Treaties," Vol. I, page 1046.

possible foreign aggression seeking undue, exclusive or
proprietary privileges in her territory, and without
foreign aid enforce an open door policy of equal opportunity to all. I am not one of those who view with
alarm the effect of the growth of China with her teem-
ing millions into a great industrial empire. I believe
that this instead of injuring foreign trade with China
would greatly increase it, and while it might change its
character in some respects, it would not diminish its
profit. A trade which depends for its profit on the
backwardness of a people in developing their own
resources and upon their inability to value at the proper
relative prices that which they have to sell and that
which they have to buy is not one which can be counted
upon as stable or permanent. . . . For the reasons I
have given, it does not seem to me that the cry of ' China
for the Chinese ' should frighten any one. All that is
meant by that is that China should devote her energies
to the development of her immense resources, to the
elevation of her industrious people, to the enlargement
of her trade and to the administrative reform of the
Empire as a great national government. Changes of
this kind would only increase our trade with her. Our
greatest export trade is with the countries most advanced
in business methods and in the development of their
particular resources. In the Philippines we have learned
that the policy which is best for the Filipinos is best in

the long run for the countries who would do business with the Islands." [11]

Besides its political importance Mr. Taft's speech is of great significance since it inaugurates a period of more vigorous participation on the part of America in the financial development of the Chinese Empire. American finance in China had up to then been singularly unsuccessful, and had met with several failures. The first instance of this kind was the failure of American financiers to obtain the contract for the construction of the Peking-Hankow line. The American group was working hard to obtain this concession. But in 1907 the Belgian Société d'Etude de Chemins de fer en Chine appeared on the scene at the right moment and with the material and moral backing of France and Russia obtained the concession in May of the same year. [12]

American financiers then formed the American-China Development Company under Mr. Calvin Brice, with the purpose of building the Hankow-Canton Railway. A contract was signed between this company and Dr. Wu Ting-Fang acting as representative of Mr. Sheng Hsuan-Huai in April, 1898. [13] The company was to provide L4,000,000. In 1899 Mr. Parsons surveyed

[11] See Millard, op. cit., page 375.
[12] See U. S. Monthly Consular Reports of 1898, Vol. LVIII, No. 218.
[13] See British Blue Books, "China," No. 1, 1899, Vol. CIX, pages 336–339.

the line. To go into the details of the contract is unnecessary since it is a dead letter to-day. For very soon a French-Belgian combination began to undermine the scheme which with the death of Mr. Brice had lost its main supporter. That the Belgians themselves ultimately suffered defeat must be ascribed in the main, according to Mr. Kent, to the course taken by the Russo-Japanese War.[14] The American element became paramount again by the influence of J. P. Morgan. Finally, however, the Huanese party, supported by the Progressives of Kuangtung, pressed for the annulment of the concession, which was arranged in September, 1905, the American Government being glad to rid itself of any further connection with a business that had been discreditable from the outset. The road was given over to the provincial authorities.

The third large scale American railroad project that remained without success was Mr. Harriman's Manchurian railroad scheme which served as forerunner to Mr. Knox's Manchurian " neutralization " scheme. A detailed account of these negotiations is given in J. O. P. Bland's book on " Recent Events and Present Policies in China," of which account we shall give a brief summary.[15]

In September, 1905, shortly after the signature of·the

14 See Kent, op. cit., pages 110 ff.
15 See Bland, op. cit., Chapter XI.

Portsmouth Treaty, Mr. E. H. Harriman proposed to Japan a joint American-Japanese ownership and working of the South Manchurian Railway. The proceedings on the side of China and Japan were, in Mr. Bland's words, " so instinct with duplicity and diplomatic sharp practice that it is impossible to form an opinion on the real merits of this peculiar question." The negotiations did not bear any fruit and nothing was heard of Mr. Harriman's scheme until 1909.

In the meanwhile the Chinese Government, represented by Tang Shao-yi, had, in 1907, arranged with Mr. W. D. Straight, United States Consul-General at Mukden, for the creation of a Manchurian Bank. This institute, financed by American capital, was to be the financial agent of the Manchurian Government, and was to undertake, together with British financiers, the construction of a line from Hsinmintung to Aigun and other important enterprises for the development of the commerce and industry of Manchuria. For the establishment of the institute a loan of $20,000,000 was intended and Messrs. Kuhn, Loeb and Co. of New York signified to the State Department at Washington their readiness to undertake to finance the Manchurian Bank. But owing to a change in China's policy following the death of the Emperor Kuang Hsu and due to Japanese obstruction the scheme fell through late in 1908.

In December of the same year negotiations were

opened at New York in regard to the Chinese Eastern
Railway which the Russian Government was willing to
sell to American financiers provided Japan would agree
to sell the South Manchurian line.   Both schemes seemed
to promise success.   But in 1909 Mr. Harriman died
and his plans died with him.

Nevertheless, Mr. Harriman's schemes had borne
fruit in so far as they served as the foundation to Mr.
Knox's scheme for the neutralization of the Manchurian
railways which was to meet with such spectacular failure.   Mr. Knox in 1909 submitted his scheme simultaneously to the British, German, Russian, Japanese and
Chinese Governments without having previously received
Russia's and Japan's acquiescence.   The whole proposition may be best illustrated by quoting Mr. Bland: [16]
" The purport of Mr. Knox's scheme amounted to a
proposal that the Powers addressed should authorize the
organization of an international syndicate to buy out the
Russian and Japanese railway interests in Manchuria.
In failing to consult Russia and Japan separately, the
Secretary of State apparently assumed that the results
of the negotiations which had taken place between the
governments of these powers and Mr. Harriman warranted him in taking their consent for granted.   Politically speaking, everything in the situation of the moment
pointed to the necessity of securing, at least, the specific

[16] See Bland, op. cit., pages 317 ff.

approval of the Russian Government on behalf of Mr. Harriman's schemes before launching the international scheme as a definite proposal. . . . The scheme as presented was a political gaffe, and the blunder was aggravated by the suggestion that, if the powers were unwilling to join in the general neutralization scheme, they should at least unite in the financing and construction of the Chinchow-Aigun Railway. In other words, if Russia and Japan were unwilling to abandon their ' special interests ' in this region, they and the other powers were invited to create new interests to compete with those of the existing railways. . . . Their suspicions thus aroused, the neutralization scheme was doomed, and the Russo-Japanese entente to divide Manchuria and Mongolia began from this moment to assume definite form and substance. Russia and Japan politely but firmly rejected Mr. Knox's proposals. . . . The immediate result of the American neutralization scheme was the Russo-Japanese agreement of the 4th of July, 1910."

Russia and Japan having rejected Mr. Knox's proposals, there is no wonder then that the Chinchow-Aigun Railway scheme was likewise doomed. " It was denounced as a deep-laid plan for attacking Russian territories in Eastern Siberia and Russia's special interests in Mongolia and Manchuria," says Bland. In recent times the southern half of it, or practically the southern half of it, has been granted to Japan by China, and now Russia has obtained the right to cover the northern section, which, however, does not exactly correspond with the route as planned originally.[17] Russia's railway is to run from Blagoveshchensk, on the left of the Amur River, to Aigun, Mergen and Harbin, with a connection between Mergen and Tsitsihar. The line gives Russia the final political dominance over her North-Manchurian sphere.

The American Government's policy was irreproachable and just. Mr. Bland calls it " a policy of righteousness, tempered by enlightened self-interest — but it required the delicate handling of a Metternich to make it effective and to dominate the equally enlightened self-interest of other powers." [18] The interests of the powers concerned happened to run in an opposite direction; their " control " in China would have been greatly diminished had the American proposal been realized. Consequently the American policy found much opposition and criticism. M. Leroy Beaulieu, the eminent French scholar, for instance, criticizes as follows: [19] " Les diverses puissances européennes ayant indiqué, sous une forme ou sous une autre, que leur attitude vis-

[17] See " Far Eastern Review," Vol. II, page 151.
[18] See Bland, op. cit., page 319.
[19] See P. Leroy Beaulieu, " Les États-Unis, Le Japon et la Russie dans le Nord Du Céleste-Empire. L'Economiste Française," March 19, 1910, page 405.

à-vis de la proposition américaine était, en définitive, subordonnée à celle des deux principaux intéressés, la cession des chemins de fer existant en Mandchourie est, aujourd'hui, une question résolue par la négative et abandonnée. Mais là ne se bornait pas l'initiative américaine. . . . La diplomatie américaine est encore un peu jeune et fruste, elle l'a montré en cette occasion, où elle a usé d'habiletés quelque peu puériles. Rendre publiques des propositions aussi graves que le rachat et la neutralisation des chemins de fer russes et japonais de Mandchourie et la construction d'une nouvelle grande ligne dans cette province, sans avoir préablement négocié avec Tokio et Saint-Petersbourg, c'était commettre un acte assurément peu aimable sinon discourtois, et c'était aggraver encore, par un manquement de forme, des dispositions qui devaient nécessairement être peu favorables au fond."

In spite of this diplomatic faux pas the world gave, nevertheless, to America credit for appreciating the dangerous situation in Manchuria and for the courage to face it. At the same time a vigorous initiative on the part of American finance helped much towards strengthening American prestige in the Orient. The Manchurian bank question marked the beginning of negotiations which led to the organization of an American group, the conclusion of the currency loan and the formation of an international syndicate. The United

States Government had recognized that it could not be of any real service to China except through its coöperation with other powers. When, therefore, in May, 1909, the British, French and German financial groups were about to conclude an agreement for the construction of the Hukuang Railways, the United States demanded admission, last not least in view of the fact that the Hukuang loan reopened the question of customs, revision in which the American Government was keenly interested.[20]   To this Willard Straight remarks:[21]   " In order, therefore, that the United States might be entitled to a practical, and not merely to a theoretical, voice in this matter, as well as to assure to American manufacturers a share in the profits of Chinese railway construction and the business arising therefrom, it was essential that representative American capitalists should participate in the Hukuang loan.   The Department of State offered this opportunity to the bankers already interested in the loan proposed by Mr. Tang Shao Yi and the American Group was organized, creating an instrument which it was hoped might enable the Administration not only to further the interests of American trade, but effectively to assist China in obtaining the consent of the powers to the customs revision she so greatly desired."

[20] See " Foreign Relations," 1909, page 160.
[21] See Straight, op. cit., page 127.

The Administration's point of view and interest in the matter finds an excellent illustration in the telegram which President Taft sent to the Prince Regent of China on July 15th, 1909. President Taft writes: " I am disturbed at the reports that there is certain prejudiced opposition to your Government's arranging for equal participation by American capital in the present railway loan. To your wise judgment it will of course be clear that the wishes of the United States are based, not only upon China's promises of 1903 and 1904, confirmed last month, but also upon broad national and impersonal principles of equity and good policy in which a regard for the best interests of your country has a prominent part. . . . I have an intense personal interest in making the use of American capital in the development of China an instrument for the promotion of the welfare of China, and an increase in her material prosperity without entanglements or creating embarrassments affecting the growth of her independent political power and the preservation of her territorial integrity."

The admission of the American group to the Hukuang loan and the various international loan negotiations will be subject matter of the following chapter. The reason for the ultimate withdrawal of the American group from the international combine, however, is a matter of strictly American policy, which therefore requires our immediate attention. The American Banking group

withdrew, due to President Wilson's refusal to continue
the moral support of the Government. In support of
his refusal, President Wilson gave in part this statement to the press: [22]   " The conditions of the loan seem
to us to touch very nearly the administrative independence of China itself; and this administration does not
feel that it ought, even by implication, to be a party to
those conditions. The responsibility on its part which
would be implied in requesting the bankers to undertake
the loan might conceivably go the length in some un-
happy contingence of forcible interference in the financial, and even the political affairs of that great Oriental
State, just now awakening to a consciousness of its
power and of its obligations to its people. The conditions include not only the pledging of particular taxes,
some of them antiquated and burdensome, to secure the
loan, but also the administration of these taxes by
foreign agents. The responsibility on the part of our
government implied in the encouragement of a loan thus
secured and administered is plain enough and is obnox-
ious to the principles upon which the government of
our people rests. . . . Our interests are those of the
open door — a door of friendship and mutual advantage.
This is the only door we care to enter."

President Wilson's objections were exclusively directed
against certain " control " provisions, which will be

[22] See Straight, op. cit., page 159.

analyzed in the following chapter. His motives were based upon the desire to be of a genuine friendship and of an ultimate benefit to China as well as to America. They expressed a high regard for the sovereign rights of China. Yet the President's action has found criticism coming from American quarters closest in contact with the Chinese situation.

Mr. Rockhill, a short time before his death, in 1914, made the following comment: [23] " Before retiring from the scene of activity in China our Government, in 1909, made one more attempt to maintain the policy of the ' open door ' and justify the expectations of the discoverers of the panacea called ' dollar diplomacy,' by securing American financial participation in several important loans which the Government of China was seeking to negotiate with various foreign banks. I will not dwell on the stirring incidents which marked the fleeting appearance of America in the field of finance and politics in China, but I cannot pass it by without mention of the permanent moral benefits it brought us, the practical assistance it rendered China while it lasted, in defending her rights and interests, and the profound regret of China and her friends when, moved by idealist views and imperfect information, the present administration at Washington saw fit, in the spring of last year, to withdraw its support from the American banks.

[23] See " Far Eastern Review," Vol. 11, page 229.

While declaring that ' our interests are those of the open door, a door of friendship and mutual advantage, this is the only door we care to enter,' it declined to take a step to show the one or to secure the other. I only know of one blow equally heavy which has been dealt our interests, our prestige, and our influence in China: it was the cancellation, in 1905, of the concession of the American-China Development Company. . . . In conclusion it seems clear to me that so long as we shut our eyes to the undoubted fact that, in the East at least, from Stamboul to Tokyo, politics, finance, and trade go hand in hand, and that neither the profits of trade can be fully reaped nor our influence and prestige be adequately upheld without incurring the responsibilities incident to political and financial activity, we must be content to play a modest, effaced rôle in the Far East, unworthy, in my opinion, of our great country and its vast interests in the Pacific."

" Dollar diplomacy," mentioned by Mr. Rockhill, has been defined by Mr. Willard D. Straight as the " logical manifestation of our national growth, and the rightful assumption by the United States of a more important place at the council table of nations. The new policy aims not only to protect those Americans already engaged in foreign trade but to promote fresh endeavor and by diplomatic action pave the way for those who have not yet been, but who will later be, obliged to sell either capital or goods abroad." [24]   Mr. Straight, representative of the American group, was a most energetic promoter of the international syndicate. He wrote in 1913: [25]   "It is to China's interest that this combination should be maintained, and it is to the interest of China as well as of the United States, that we should retain our present position therein. China's great problem to-day is that of finance. It is to her advantage that we are entitled to a practical voice in its solution, and it is to the advantage of American trade that the United States continue to be an active party in Chinese loan negotiations."

A similar stand has been taken by the American Association.[26]   "The policy of the United States Government in discouraging the investment of American capital in Chinese railways and in loans to the Republic has been detrimental to our merchants, but as the administration gains a clearer view of the situation in China and begins to recognize the things that must be done if the United States is to share in this vast trade area, there are possibilities of some modifications of this policy which is believed to have been put forth without sufficient investigation and, at that, on sentimental grounds. This Association should use every means in its power to awaken the Government in Washington through

[24] See Straight, op. cit., page 121.
[25] See Straight op. cit., page 157.
[26] See "Far Eastern Review," Vol. 11, page 360.

whatever means it can find, to the necessity for a more vigorous policy in China to secure for us and to hold open when secured as liberal advantages for the extension of our trade as are now enjoyed by other nationalities."

Meanwhile American finance, under the leadership of the American International Corporation, has attempted to undertake developments in China independently and without government support. In doing so the Corporation wanted to avoid transactions clothed with any political character, adhering strictly to business lines. In their recent contracts for railways in Central China the American financiers propose to proceed on a new basis.[27] The Chinese Government was to remain owner of the lines constructed and would issue the bonds. Since the Chinese have not as yet a sufficient number of engineers and technical railway men to construct and operate the lines arrangements were to be made whereby the Chinese Government will secure the services of American experts to assist them in the management of the new roads. For services in financing and in directing operation the Corporation would receive a certain percentage of the profits in operation.

The latest developments indicate a return of the United States Government to the policy of approving loans by American bankers to China.[28] The bankers will give

[27] See *Journal of the American Asiatic Association*, Vol. XVI, No. 12, pages 373 ff.
[28] See New York *Times*, July 30, 1918.

assurance " that they will coöperate with the Government and follow the policies outlined by the Department of State." While the Government assures " that, if the terms and conditions of the loan are accepted by this Government and by the Government to which the loan is made, in order to encourage and facilitate the free intercourse between American citizens and foreign states which is mutually advantageous, the Government will be willing to aid in every way possible and to make prompt and vigorous representations and to take every possible step to insure the execution of equitable contracts made in good faith by its citizens in foreign lands." It is also " hoped that the American group will be associated with bankers of Great Britain, Japan and France."

A very important point is the hoped for financial coöperation between the United States and Japan. The American-Japanese agreement of November 2, 1917, bids fair to be the foundation for a financial coöperation between the two countries in China.[29] It has removed, in the words of Mr. Lansing, " a feeling of suspicion as to the motives inducing the activities of the other in the Far East, a feeling which, if unchecked, promised to develop a serious situation."

The two governments furthermore explicitly " deny that they have any purpose to infringe in any way the

[29] See end of Chapter " Japan."

independence or territorial integrity of China, and they declare furthermore that they will always adhere to the principles of the so-called ' open door ' or equal opportunity for commerce and industry in China." In fact, the reaffirmation of the " open door " policy and the introduction of a principle of non-interference with the sovereignty and territorial integrity of China are reassuring factors in the Far Eastern Question for the reason that both Japan and the United States, by this declaration, bind themselves to see that China will obtain a fair deal, not only at the hands of other nations, but from themselves as well.

CHAPTER VIII

INTERNATIONAL CONTROL

INTERNATIONAL financial competition in China, with its struggle for " spheres of interest," and national " control," has during later years gradually given way to international coöperation and international control. An Anglo-German agreement between the Hongkong-Shanghai Bank and the Deutsch-Asiatische Bank for mutual participation in administrative and railway loans to China had, as we have seen, existed previous to the " battle of concessions." The first financial transactions done in common under this agreement were the two Chino-Japanese War indemnity loans of 1896 and 1898, of L16,000,-000 each, which were paralleled by a Franco-Russian loan of 400,000,000 francs of 1895.[1] All three loans were secured by the Maritime Customs Revenue administered by the International Maritime Customs Service.[2] The Russo-French loan enjoyed an additional guarantee from the Russian Government while the Anglo-German loan of 1898 was charged upon certain additional likin revenues which were also collected by the International

[1] See " China Year Book," 1913, page 332.
[2] See Chapter I.

Maritime Customs Service. To this the British Representative refers under March 18, 1898, as follows:[3]
"The only point of other than financial or commercial
interest is the provision for the placing under the control
of the Inspector-General of Maritime Customs the likin
revenues pledged as security, for this may have important future results, as in the case of every other measure
likely to benefit their country, the Chinese Government
has refused to take this step until forced thereto by
necessity."

Under the part control of the Maritime Customs Service falls furthermore the Boxer Indemnity-Service, since
payments are secured upon the balance of the revenues
of the Maritime Customs after payment of preëxisting
charges, upon the Native Customs Revenues at open
ports, and the Salt Gabelle.[4] The amortization was to
commence the first of January, 1902, payable annually,
and shall be finished at the end of the year 1940. The
Anglo-German loan of 1898 was followed in February,
1905, by the final exchange-adjustment of the Boxer
Indemnity, amounting to L1,000,000 and secured by the
Peking octroi and Shansi likin.[5]

That the collection of the revenues upon which these
first three international loans and the Boxer Indemnity
were pledged fell under foreign "control" was, as we

[3] See British Blue Books, "China," No. CIX, 1899, No. 59.
[4] See "China Year Book," 1913, page 333.
[5] *Ibidem.*

have seen due to the fact that the Maritime Customs were at that time under foreign expert supervision. This supervision had become a stable and well founded institution and was generally recognized as a source of great benefit to foreigners as well as to Chinese. Few difficulties were therefore encountered when these loan services thus fell automatically under foreign " control." But the case was entirely different with " control " embodied in the various railroad agreements, the first of which was that made by the Chinese Government in 1898, with the British and Chinese Corporation, for a loan to the Imperial Railways of North China. The control stipulations of most of the railroad agreements were exceedingly severe, as we have demonstrated in the preceding chapters. The lenders, besides securing a first mortgage on the railways, were entitled to a share in the profits and the management of the lines. This form of " control " was naturally a great blow to Chinese pride and it therefore found considerable opposition from many quarters. The first international railway loan agreement now altered conditions substantially. This was the Anglo-German Tientsin-Pukow loan agreement concluded in 1908 by the same banks which had arranged the indemnity loans of 1896, 1898 and 1902.

The signature of the Tientsin-Pukow agreement, says Mr. Straight,[6] " marked the first recognition by the

[6] See Straight, op. cit., page 132.

banks of the increasing efficiency of the ' Young China party. These men demanded the radical modification of the old loan terms. They considered ' control ' subversive of China's sovereign rights and, flattered by the blandishments of rival foreign interests, they were determined to exact from the world a consideration similar to that accorded Japan after years of patriotic self-sacrifice and conscientious endeavor. The avowed purpose of these officials to weaken the hold of the foreigner on China was heartily applauded throughout the provinces. It served as a patriotic issue on which an appeal could be made to the masses and a cloak under which the provincial gentry could cover their real purpose, which was to restrict the extension of the Peking Government's authority by railways built with foreign loans, or otherwise, and their determination that if foreign loans were made, the chances for peculation should not be monopolized by the metropolitan mandarins."

The agreement of January 13th, 1908,[7] sanctioned the flotation of a loan of L5,000,000 at five per cent. issued to the Chinese at 93 and to the public at 98¾ for a term of 30 years, repayment to commence at the end of 10 years. Of the total loan L1,850,000 was issued by the Hongkong and Shanghai Bank and L3,150,000 by the Deutsch-Asiatische Bank. The line was accordingly

[7] See "Far Eastern Review," Supplement, Nov., 1909, for text of the Agreement.

subdivided in two sections. The northern portion from Tientsin extended to the Grand Canal, a distance of 385 miles, and was built by German capital. The southern portion extended from the Grand Canal to Pukow, 236½ miles, and was built by British capital. According to Article 9 the loan is secured by a first charge upon likin and internal revenues of Chihli, Shantung, and Kiangsu Provinces, amounting to a total of 3,800,000 Haikwan taels a year.

Regarding administration or "control" of the line, Article 17 of the agreement provides that: "The construction and control of the railway will be entirely in the hands of the Imperial Chinese Government. For the work of the northern and southern sections respectively the Chinese Government will select and appoint fully qualified German and British Chief Engineers, acceptable to the syndicate. These two Chief Engineers shall be under the orders of the Managing Director, or his duly authorized representative, and will carry out all the wishes of the Railway Administration with regard to the plan and construction of the line. They must pay all due respect to the Director General and the Managing Director. The terms of their respective agreements will be arranged by the Director General on his sole authority."

To ensure Chinese control after completion Article I concludes: "On the completion of the line the Imperial

Chinese Government will appoint an Engineer-in-Chief, who during the period of the loan shall be a European without reference to the syndicate."

By 1910 the money was exhausted and it became necessary to raise a supplementary loan of L4,800,000, divided into two equal parts, to complete the work.

In the Tientsin-Pukow Agreement of 1908, it was for the first time stipulated, that in case of default on the loan service, the hypothecated revenues should be administered by the Maritime Customs Service. The principle of joint management was abandoned. No authority was conferred by the Tientsin-Pukow contract upon the auditors of the banks to stop the withdrawal of funds in case the Chinese officials were found guilty of peculation.

" These terms," says the *Far Eastern Review,* " were distinctly favorable to China, and the precedent set has been seized upon and will be used to obtain better terms in future agreements. The Board of Posts and Communications are convinced that the management of roads should be in the hands of the Government. And in the hands of the Government they should be exceedingly profitable, though everything depends not only upon sagacious management, but upon scrupulous treatment of earnings. The European bankers' sole and only object in endeavoring in the past to obtain supervision over railway management and finance was to see to it that all moneys were honestly dealt with and the interests of bondholders protected. The opponents of what are now described as 'the Tientsin-Pukow terms' declare that the way has been deliberately left open for ruthless squandering and peculation in railway funds. It is therefore all the more incumbent upon the railway administration to demonstrate to the world that they are capable of controlling their officials and the funds that are destined to pass through their hands." [8]

The Chinese officials, however, did not fulfill the expectations and trust placed in them. Mr. Straight informs us that: [9] "from the commencement of the construction of this line there have been numerous scandals, the most flagrant instance resulting in the degradation of the director general and a number of his subordinates. The cost of construction has far exceeded even the most liberal estimates, and the loan service will therefore constitute a heavy charge on the revenues of the line."

"Owing to the unsatisfactory operation of the so-called 'Tientsin-Pukow' terms," continues Mr. Straight, "negotiations were conducted in the winter of 1908-1909 between the British, German and French Groups and their respective Governments with a view to reaching an understanding as to the degree of 'control' to

[8] See "Far Eastern Review," Vol. IX, page 336.
[9] See Straight, op. cit., page 133.

be demanded from China as a condition precedent to future loans." These negotiations were for a loan to construct both the Canton-Hankow and Hankow-Szechuan line or, as they are called collectively, the Hukuang Railways. At first it was intended that there should be Anglo-American coöperation; but America refused to have anything to do with the project in 1904. Later on, in 1905, France and England came to an arrangement with regard to this line. Little, however, was done until, in 1908, the German group insisted upon participation in said enterprise.[10] Diplomatic protest and recriminations followed owing to the willingness of the Germans to agree to " Tientsin-Pukow " terms, while the British insisted upon more effective " control." [11] The controversies finally resulted in a compromise under which the British and French associates combined with the German group to negotiate the Hukuang loan jointly. The agreement was initialed on the sixth day of June, 1909, and the " control " provisions accepted by the banks were similar to those embodied in the Tientsin-Pukow Agreement, as we shall see presently.

At this point the United States interfered. The American legation in Peking forwarded a protest to the Grand Councilor, Chang Chih Tung, against the rati-

[10] See Chapter II (72).
[11] See Straight, op. cit., page 133.

fication of the preliminary agreement on the ground
that American financiers had secured, in 1904, a promise
from the Chinese Government that in the event of the
floating of foreign loans for the Hupeh section of the
Szechuan road China would consult first the United
States and Great Britain.[12] Inasmuch as the United
States had not officially relinquished her right to participation, the American Government now demanded admission of an American group composed of Messrs. J. P.
Morgan and Co., Kuhn, Loeb and Co., the First National
Bank, and The National City Bank, all of New York.
The group was represented by Mr. Willard D. Straight.
Mr. Knox supported his demand by pointing to the
" menace to foreign trade likely to ensue from the lack
of proper sympathy between the powers most vitally
interested in the preservation of the principle of equality
of commercial opportunity," adding that " the Government of the United States regards full and frank
coöperation as best calculated to maintain the open door
and the integrity of China and . . . that the formation
of a powerful American, British, French and German
financial group would further that end." [13]

It was last not least due to the personal interference
of President Taft,[14] that the Chinese agreed to provide
for equal participation of America in the railway loan,

[12] See " Foreign Relations," 1909 (Vol. 5704), pages 144 ff.
[13] See " Foreign Relations," 1909 (Vol. 5704), page 152.
[14] See preceding chapter.

and that " Tripartite Banks " consequently invited the American group, in May, 1910, to join them in the combination which they had effected the year before. This invitation was accepted and an intergroup agreement was signed in November, 1910.[15] The final agreement for the Hukuang loan was signed with China by representatives of the four nation syndicate on May 20th, 1911, on which day the preliminary agreement of June, 1909, was sanctioned with the addition of a few provisions referring to American participation, and an increase of the amount to L6,000,000.[16]

The Imperial Chinese Government Five Per Cent. Hukuang Railway's Sinking Fund Gold Loan of L6,000,000 was to the amount of L500,000 for the redemption at a premium of $2\frac{1}{2}$ per cent. of certain unredeemed Gold Bonds of the total par value of $2,222,000, issued by the American China Development Company on behalf of the Chinese Government, and the balance for the construction of a government railway in the Provinces of Hunan, Hupeh, and Szechuan, comprising two sections: 1. The Hupeh-Hunan section of the Canton-Hankow Railway, being a line from Wuchang south through Yochow and Changsha to a point on the

[15] See " Far Eastern Review," Vol. XIII, page 83.
[16] For the text see " Far Eastern Review," Supplement, Aug., 1911. See also U. S. Daily Consular Reports, Oct. 20, 1913, No. 245. For the preliminary agreement of 1909 see " Foreign Relations," 1909, pages 152 and 200.

southern boundary of Hunan, there connecting with the Kwangtung section. This section of a total length of 900 kilometers is under a British engineer in chief. 2. The Hupeh section of the Hankow-Szechuan line, from Kwangshui, on the Peking-Hankow line, through Siangyang and Chingmen to Ichang, 600 kilometers under a German engineer in chief, and from Ichang to Kweichowfu in Szechuan, 300 kilometers under an American engineer in chief. The question of control is regulated in Article XVII: " The construction and control of the railway lines shall be entirely and exclusively vested in the Imperial Chinese Government. For the work of construction the Imperial Chinese Government will select for appointment a fully qualified British Engineer-in-Chief for the Hupeh-Hunan section of the Canton-Hankow railway line to Yichangshien, and a fully qualified German Engineer-in-Chief for the Kwangshui-Ichang section of the Szechuan-Hankow railway line, with a fully qualified American Engineer-in-Chief for the section of that line from Ichang to Kweichowfu, at the same time informing the Banks of the selection made." At Kweichow the system was to connect with the future Kweichow-Chungking-Chengtu section of over 500 miles which had been reserved for French capital, as no share of the construction of the system provided for by the Hukuang agreement was

allotted to the French group.[17]   Article XVIII concedes
to the British and Chinese Corporation and the Deutsch-
Asiatische Bank the exclusive purchasing rights for the
entire system, including the American section, on which
they are allowed a purchasing commission of five pei
cent.   There is, however, a gentleman's compact between
the four groups of May 23rd, 1910, that fair play will
be observed and that the purchasing agents will " make
all proper provision for the receipt on an absolute basis
of equality of tenders from British, German, French,
and American manufacturers." [18]

The loan of six million pound sterling was according
to Article IX secured in respect to both principal and
interest, as a first charge upon Hupeh and Hunan provincial salt and likin revenues and Hupeh rice tax amounting to a total of 5,200,000 Haikwan taels a year.   These
revenues are declared free from all other loans, charges
or mortgages.   It is furthermore stipulated that " so
long as principal and interest of this Loan are regularly
paid, there shall be no interference with these Provincial
revenues; but if principal or interest of the Loan be in
default at due date, then, after a reasonable period of
grace, likin and other suitable internal revenues of the
Provinces of Hupeh and Hunan sufficient to provide the

[17] See Chapter IV; see also " Far Eastern Review," Vol. 9, page
305.
[18] See " Foreign Relations," 1910, page 283.

amounts above stated shall forthwith be transferred to, and administered by, the Imperial Maritime Customs in the interests of the bondholders."

The bankers had acquiesced in these lenient control provisions, " feeling that the punishment inflicted after the Tientsin-Pukow frauds and the surveillance of the National Assembly over the expenditure of loan funds, as well as the difficulties by which the central government was confronted, justified them in confirming the " control " provisions of the original agreement." [19] That the Chinese, on the other hand, were able to secure " Tientsin-Pukow " terms in the original Hukuang agreement — despite the fact that more stringent control was needed — was due to the rivalry between the British and German groups. The international syndicate was furthermore confronted by an ever increasing " anti-loan " agitation in the provinces through which the Hukuang lines were to be constructed, which obliged Chang Chih Tung — especially in the face of the opposition by the National Assembly — to adhere as strictly as possible to the terms of the original contract. But notwithstanding the multitude of good reasons for a lenient " control " the bankers should soon be forced to have the security revised, the arrangements for the banking of funds reconsidered and a change instituted with regard to the auditors. It was the Chinese revolution

[19] See Straight, op. cit., page 135.

which necessitated the reconsideration of several points in the agreement. Says the *Far Eastern Review*,[20] " At the time the agreement was being negotiated an effort was made to have the railway lines to be built pledged as collateral security, but the authorities resisted overtures in this regard chiefly owing to the popular opposition to placing what are described as ' sovereign rights ' in the hands of the foreigners. The revolution produced such changes in the value of the security already pledged, however, that reconsideration was necessary. One of the first steps to be taken by the revolutionists was to declare the abolition of likin, and though that was eventually revised likin collections fell off almost entirely as a result of the dislocation of the machinery of tax collection. Other revenues pledged also suffered. . . . The Government protested that the taxes were unaffected, but after much argument it was agreed that the property and materials of the lines should be specially given as a provisional guarantee that the likin was unimpaired." In Article 14 it was stipulated that certain funds should be placed with certain Chinese banks. The credit of all native banks being seriously affected through the revolution the Chinese Government and the representatives of the " Quadruple Banks " arranged in 1913 that the loan funds should be deposited in the Hongkong and Shanghai Bank, Deutsch-Asiatische Bank, Banque

20 " Far Eastern Review," Vol. IX, page 454.

de l'Indo-Chine, and the International Banking Corporation, instead of with the native banks.[21] Finally China undertook of her own accord to engage experienced foreign accountants for the various railway sections.

The construction of the Hukuang railways had made but little progress owing to the political and financial state of China during and following the revolution, which was unfavorable to railway construction. The revolution has also set a halt to the issue of the socalled Currency Loan. On April 15th, 1911, an agreement had been signed between the President of the Ministry of Finance on behalf of China, with the " Four-Power " syndicate, authorizing the issue by the foreign bankers of a Five Per Cent. Sinking Fund Gold Loan for an aggregate amount of L10,000,000. The issue price of this loan was to be 95, and of the L9,500,000 which was actually to be handed over to the Chinese Government, L1,000,000 was earmarked for the industrial development of Manchuria, while L8,500,000 were to be devoted to the reform of a chaotic currency that had always been at the root of China's financial troubles.[22] The loan was to be secured on certain revenues appertaining to the three Manchurian provinces, and on a recently imposed surtax upon salt.

[21] See " China Year Book," 1914, page 234.
[22] See " China Year Book," 1912, page 288.

The question of "control" should prove again the greatest stumbling block in the path of negotiations. To quote Mr. Straight: [23] "Practically the only loans previously falling" within this category ("government" or "administrative" loans) had been required to pay indemnities abroad and there was no necessity therefore that the lenders should exercise "control" over their expenditure. The currency loan, however, was to carry out a definite program and not for general administrative purposes. The four banking groups now acting in harmony believed some form of supervision to be necessary, and it was thought that the "control" machinery devised for railway loans, could, with certain modifications be utilized for assuring the proper applications of the borrowed funds under the currency reform program.

"The Chinese had reluctantly agreed to various control provisions in railway loan agreements, but they feared that to admit the principle of supervision over administrative expenditures would be to pave the way for foreign control over China's general finances. An arrangement was finally made, however, whereby China submitted to the groups her program of currency reform for their acceptance, and agreed to expend the loan funds only in accordance therewith, to publish quarterly reports of disbursements made, and to engage a foreign expert to assist the Bureau of Currency Reform.

[23] See Straight, op. cit., page 135.

" The Loan has not been issued but it is open to question whether this ' control,' in practice, would have prevented peculation, and insured the proper expenditure of loan funds, and the effective operation of the currency reform program."

So much for the international loans preceding the revolution. At the outbreak of the revolution in October, 1911, the Empire faced an annual deficit variously estimated from twenty to seventy million taels.[24]   The imperial authorities at Peking soon realized that the scarcity of funds made offensive military operations impossible.   Their general inability to cope with the situation, together with their loss of revenue from the revolted provinces, capture of Government funds, and the wholesale embezzlement of moneys by officials, brought them face to face with bankruptcy.   Various foreign sources were therefore approached regarding loans to the imperial Government: a Baron Cottu for francs 150,000,000, certain American financiers for L1,000,000, on the security of the Peking-Kalgan Railway, a British-Belgian-French Syndicate under Russian influence for taels 90,000,000, Germany for $20,000,000, and last not least the " Four-Power " Syndicate for various sums. The Provincial Assemblies and Republicans in the South

[24] The financial history of the Revolution is given in the Chinese Year Books of 1913 and 1914 and has also been recorded by George Bronson Rea in the " Far Eastern Review," Vols. VIII and IX, *passim.*

immediately raised an outcry against any possible loans, threatening a boycott against the nations furnishing the funds. This caused the bankers to hesitate and consult with their Governments through their respective legations. The foreign legations in Peking were at that time in favor of the North. In view of the fact that the British interests predominated in China, the Powers deferred to the wishes of Great Britain in saying whether the Manchus and Yuan Shih Kai should receive financial support or not. And it was " generally understood that up to this juncture, the British Minister at Peking, Sir John Jordan, fully agreed with his colleagues in that Yuan, as the only man to save the situation, should receive foreign financial aid." [25] But " to the repeated recommendations of the legations in support of Yuan, the Chancellors answered that as the South was entirely under Republican rule, any support to the North would result in retaliatory trade boycotts, destruction of property, and possible anti-foreign uprisings, with consequent massacre of all foreigners in the interior. In view of this, the Governments could not sanction any financial assistance to the other side, and China would have to solve its internal problem unaided." [26] The neutrality proclamation of the powers following shortly afterwards sealed the doom of the Manchu Government,

[25] See " Far Eastern Review," Vol. 8, page 345.
[26] See " Far Eastern Review," Vol. 8, page 345.

the collapse of their loan negotiations convincing them
of the hopelessness of their cause.

But the powers, in pursuance of their policy of maintaining strict neutrality, would not countenance loans
to the Revolutionary Government. The latter was
therefore compelled to close a deal with Japan, which
Power was ready to widen her interests in China, and
accordingly prepared to sign the agreement for the
hypothecation of the properties of the China Merchants'
Steam Navigation Company. But, " When the great
British shipping and commercial companies realized that
their interests were in danger and the Republicans were
playing into the hands of their formidable Japanese
rivals, who by securing a lien on the China Merchants'
properties would be masters of the river and coastwise
shipping trade, then the law of self-preservation over-
shadowed all other considerations, and the demand was
made on the British financial group to break the deadlock and advance the funds to Sun Yat-sen, to prevent
the China Merchants' Steam Navigation Company passing into the control of the Japanese. And the British
group with the support of its Government acted." [27]

At that time the Chinese situation had been cleared
up considerably. The Manchus abdicated on Feb. 12th
and the Chinese Government was consolidated under the
leadership of Yuan Shih Kai with the active support

[27] See " Far Eastern Review," Vol. 8, page 374.

from Sun Yat-sen and the South. Immediately there-after the proposition was made to the Quadruple Syndicate that the embargo on foreign loans be raised and permission given to advance funds to the new government. To this the syndicate agreed and on Feb. 28, 1912, the Hongkong and Shanghai Banking Corporation, acting on behalf of the quartette, made an advance of taels 2,000,000 to the Chinese Government at Nanking — last not least stirred to action by the British shipping interests, as suggested above.

The deadlock had been raised on the previous day, i.e., on Feb. 27th, when the representatives of the syndicate at the invitation of Mr. Tang Shao Yi, representing the republican government, discussed with him the question of a general Reorganization Loan. According to Mr. Straight " Mr. Tang stated the immediate requirements of the Chinese Government, and requested the representatives to ask their groups to finance the same. In addition he discussed the Chinese revenues available as security for a large loan to reorganize the Chinese Administration, and to initiate a scheme of commercial and industrial development. He asked the representatives how much China could borrow on this security, and finally, himself suggested the figure of L60,000,000 which he wished the banks to loan in five annual installments of L12,000,000 each." [28] As security for the

[28] See Straight, op. cit., page 157.

proposed advances he offered to issue sterling treasury bills, to be secured as a secondary charge upon the Salt Gabelle. The advance of taels 2,000,000 of the following day was made at Mr. Tang's request to meet the urgent requirements of the Nanking authorities.

Negotiations for further advances were proceeding when the Peking mutiny, followed by similar outbreaks in other parts of the North, threatened to involve the whole of the North in anarchy. It was not until March 2nd that the situation in Peking was once more in hand, and on that day the syndicate was requested to make further advances. To this request the bankers agreed, making an advance of taels 1,100,000 on March 7th. On March 9th the syndicate received a letter from the President which is of particular importance in the light of subsequent events.

According to this letter, it was understood and agreed [29] "That the banks hold a firm option for the provision of the further monthly requirements of the Chinese Government for the months of March, April, May, June and possibly July and August, which the Four Groups have already been requested to finance, against the delivery of additional sterling Treasury Bills on terms to be arranged.

"That in consideration of the assistance rendered by the groups to China in the present emergency, and

[29] See "China Year Book," 1913, page 350.

of their services in supporting her credit on the foreign markets, the Chinese Government assures to the groups (provided their terms are equally advantageous with those otherwise obtainable) the firm option of undertaking the comprehensive loan for general reorganization purposes, already proposed to them, to be floated as soon as possible, and to be applied in the first instance to the redemption of the sterling Treasury Bills aforesaid."

Every arrangement had been made by the groups to continue the payment of the advances agreed upon, when on March 14th they received definite information that the Premier Tang Shao-Yi was negotiating with a nominally Belgian Syndicate for an independent loan. And despite the protests of the Groups, Premier Tang signed the loan on March 14th, subject to the confirmation of the National Assembly at Nanking. The European Syndicate which undertook the loan consisted of the Eastern Bank Ltd. and Messrs. J. Henry Schröder and Co., both of London, Messrs. A. Spitzer and Co., Paris, The Russo-Asiatic Bank and a Belgian Group composed of La Société Générale de Belgique, La Banque Sino-Belge, and La Société Belge de Chemins de Fer en Chine. The agreement provided for a loan of L1,000,000 at five per cent., issued at 97 (ninety-seven) and redeemable in 12 months, to be followed subsequently by a larger loan, amounting in all to L10,000,000.

It was according to Article LV secured upon the general revenues and specifically upon the property and revenue of the Peking-Kalgan Railway.[30] " The Chinese Government shall deposit with the Bank, Government Treasury Bills for one million pounds sterling in amounts of ten thousand pounds each. The Bills shall be secured by the general revenue of the State, and the payment of the principal and interest is further secured by a first mortgage on the net income and property of the Peking-Kalgan railway." The article of greatest significance is No. 15: " In consideration of the financial assistance given by the Bank (Banque Sino-Belge) to the Government under this agreement, the Government engages to give a preference to the Bank for such loan or loans (future loans) until an aggregate amount of ten million pounds sterling shall have been floated through the Bank provided the terms offered are equally advantageous to those offered by other parties."

A comparison of these terms, signed on March 14th with the terms of the agreement signed by President Yuan on March 9th, reveals a concession of preferential rights to both parties, or in other words a breach of the earlier contract. According to the *Far Eastern Review* this would indicate: " that the new rulers of China adhered to the traditional tactics of playing one group against the other in the hope that by such com-

[30] See " China Year Book," 1913, page 351.

petition China would free herself from any foreign monopoly or control of her finances." [31]   The premier himself gave for an explanation that he was forced to arrange the Belgian loan because of an — alleged — refusal of the Quadruple Syndicate to make the advances he required.[32]   But the only true justification for China's action is to be found in the fact that the price paid by the bankers for the Belgian loan was lower than that which the four groups were ready to give.

In addition to the breach of faith the pledging of the revenues and property of the Peking-Kalgan Railway was regarded by the four governments concerned as a violation of the Anglo-French Peking-Hankow Railway Redemption Loan of 1908 and of the engagement entered into by Great Britain and China in 1902 that the Peking-Kalgan Railway should not be mortgaged for a foreign loan.[33]

It must be remarked, in this connection, that there is every reason to believe that the loan, although termed a Belgian one, was in fact a Russian affair, for the syndicate is identical with that formed by Russia for participation in the " Six-Power Syndicate." The possible political character of this loan is, according to the *Far Eastern Review,* made clear when it is remembered that Russia had for years endeavored to gain control

[31] See " Far Eastern Review," Vol. 8, page 378.
[32] See " China Year Book," 1913, page 353.
[33] See " China Year Book," 1913, page 353.

of a railway across Mongolia and through the Kalgan Pass to the capital.[34]

Furthermore, the signature of the Belgian loan, as Mr. Straight remarks, " affected the security for the large loan which the groups had been asked to undertake — and it carried no guarantee whatsoever that the funds furnished or to be furnished would be properly expended, it increased China's liabilities without insuring any increase in the effectiveness of her administration and instead of rehabilitating, it was calculated to prejudice her credit." [35]

For all these reasons the Four-Power Syndicate immediately suspended further payments, and refused to comply with their side of the agreement unless the so-called " Belgian " loan was canceled. In their protest against this loan and their demand for its cancellation the bankers found the active support of their respective governments under the leadership of Great Britain. The London Foreign Office had put itself on record as opposed to any loan coming from sources other than the Quadruple Syndicate, when it refused its support to the British Banks which had taken an interest in the Belgian loan. On March 14, the Foreign Office assured the Hongkong and Shanghai Bank of its exclusive support during the loan negotiations, when requested to do so by said

[34] See " Far Eastern Review," Vol. 8, page 379.
[35] See Straight, op. cit., page 140.

Bank.[36]   The justification of the Foreign Office for this support was that any other loan " might interfere with the temporary arrangements made for financing the Chinese Provisional Government, or . . . might conflict with the terms or weaken the security of the large loan for reorganization purposes, which your bank and the allied French, German, and American groups are negotiating, with the full knowledge of their Governments."   The Foreign Office likewise recognizes " that they are under obligation not only to the Hongkong and Shanghai Bank, but also to the governments and groups concerned in these advances, not to give their support to any other group in negotiating with the Chinese Government any loan as described above until the large loan out of which these advances and the expenses of reorganization are to be covered has been successfully negotiated, and, above all, until the security on which it is to be issued has been definitely settled."

The standpoint of the English Foreign Office is also expressed in the following dispatch: " His Majesty's Government and the other governments concerned have, from the experience of past years, come to the unanimous conclusion that, both in the interests of their own financiers and investing public, and also as a safeguard of China's credit, it is incumbent on them to prevent, as far

[36] See British Blue Books, " China," No. 2, 1912, Vol. CXXI, No. 1, ff.

as lies in their power, all possibility of a return to the former dangerous policy of unprofitable international competition in China, which only enabled the Chinese Government to obtain money without adequate guarantees, and rendered it impossible for the governments interested to exercise the necessary control over the terms of any loans. There can be no doubt that the internationalization of future loans would go far to secure this desirable end." [37]

To enforce the broadest possible internationalization of Chinese loans, the syndicate decided at this time to strengthen its position by inviting the coöperation of Russian and Japanese financiers. By this step it was hoped to secure the absolute unanimity among the six Powers possessing the most substantial interests in China, to prevent the entrance of unscrupulous financiers and the dissipation, by reckless and unchecked borrowing, of the nation's tangible securities. Japan at once accepted the invitation and designated the Yokohama Specie Bank as the official institution through which her share of the loans would be negotiated. After a long hesitation, Russia also signified her willingness to enter the combination, " although it has been quite apparent that she desired to play a lone hand and push her advantage through the medium of the Belgo-Russian financial

[37] See " China," No. 2, 1912, Vol. CXXI, No. 7.

syndicate." [38]   Russian interests were to be represented by the Russo-Asiatic Bank in coöperation with the same syndicate as had undertaken the " Belgian " loan.

The " Belgian " loan had meanwhile been canceled upon the strong representations by the foreign ministers, and the negotiations between the bankers and Mr. Tang were resumed on May 3rd. The question of control arose immediately. To appreciate the difficulties the bankers were obliged to take into consideration, we shall avail ourselves of a summary of the situation existing at this time, as given by Mr. Straight. [39]

" They (the six groups) had been requested by China to furnish roughly 10,000,000 taels or L1,300,000 a month for six months and to provide other sums, making the aggregate amount to be advanced 80,000,000 taels or about L10,000,000.

" It would have been impossible to issue a Chinese loan at this time except at a figure so low as to prejudice the quotations for Chinese bonds already on the market, in the hands of the public not of the groups. To furnish the sums immediately required therefore the banks would have been obliged to discount treasury bills, which they would have either had to hold themselves, or dispose of to a very limited clientele.

[38] See " Far Eastern Review," Vol. VIII, page 381.
[39] Straight, op. cit., pages 142 ff.

" These advances were required to pay the army, to finance the disbandment of superfluous troops, and to meet the current expenses of the government. The large loan was to be expended to redeem the treasury bills, to clear off arrears in China's indemnity and loan services, and to meet certain pressing outstanding obligations. Mr. Tang proposed to use the balance to make up the loss of likin, which he desired immediately to abolish, pending the consent of the powers to an increase in the customs tariff. In addition he had certain vague schemes for railway construction, afforestation, and the establishment of mills of various sorts.

" For the advances and large loan requested the Chinese Government proposed to pledge the Salt Gabelle as security. The service of the Boxer Indemnity is a first charge on this revenue. It was estimated, however, that it now yields taels 47,000,000 per annum and could be increased to at least half as much again if honestly collected.

" The Chinese Government at this time was powerless to collect the taxes which it offered as security and was unable to meet its indemnity and loan payments, to pay troops or to finance its current administrative expenses and its permanence was by no means assured.

" During the course of the negotiations, from February to June, the Chinese officials had shown little appreciation of the magnitude of their financial task and had evinced little ability in dealing effectively therewith.

" The groups nevertheless had advanced 12,100,000 taels in order to enable the administration to meet its most urgent needs and to prevent the disorders and mutinies which it was feared would occur unless funds, which the Government could not secure from its own people, were obtained.

" These advances had been made subject to certain conditions to insure their proper application to the purposes for which they were borrowed, yet the Chinese officials charged with their expenditure had placed every obstacle in the way of a proper and efficient audit, to which they had agreed.

" Patriotic Chinese, proud of their Republic and hopeful and confident of its future, may regret the necessity of including such facts in this statement. These men, however, if they be fair minded, must admit that the banking groups, no matter how friendly they might be to China, would not have been warranted in disregarding them.

" Because of these facts the groups were unwilling to undertake the business without the joint support of their respective governments. Because of these facts, moreover, they deemed it possible to proceed with advances and to undertake the reorganization loan only on certain conditions, which were briefly as follows:

" 1. That the groups should have the right to satisfy

themselves as to purposes for which funds were required.

" 2. That China should herself create a system of audit in which foreigners should be employed with powers not merely advisory, but also executive so as to ensure the effective expenditure of loan funds borrowed for the purposes specified.

" 3. That the salt taxes to be hypothecated for the service of this loan should be administered either by the existing Maritime Customs organization or by a separate Chinese service like the customs, however, under foreign direction, thus safeguarding the proper administration of the security despite the possible continuation or recurrence of unsettled conditions in China.

" 4. That the groups should take the first series of the loan of L60,000,000, at a fixed price, and be assured an option on the subsequent series at a price to be based on the market quotation of the first issue, thus giving China the benefit of any improvement in her credit.

" 5. That to protect the quotation of bonds issued and to assure a successful marketing of subsequent series China should not borrow through other groups until the entire loan of L60,000,000 had been issued.

" 6. That for a period of five years China should appoint the groups financial agents to assist the administration in its work of reorganization.

" These conditions were submitted to the Chinese Government and in reply the group representatives in Peking were informed that it would be impossible to China to accept a loan on such terms. Negotiations, however, though interrupted, were not formally broken off, and from the end of June discussions were continued between the Chinese officials and the group representatives, but without result.

" The difficulty was not a question of the price at which the bankers should take the bonds. It was the question of 'control.' The Chinese particularly objected to placing the Salt Gabelle under the Maritime Customs, or any foreign directed service, and to the creation of a proper audit department to appointing the groups financial agents."

The strongest opposition came from the Chinese Government itself. The premier declined to entertain any proposal for effective supervision, and hinted that in the event of the bankers pressing their proposals, he would suspend negotiations and endeavor to raise money by means of a poll-tax, or some similar method. At secret sessions of the National Council it appeared that the council was also strongly opposed to any form of foreign control, and this feeling was reflected in the provinces, where a popular clamor was voiced against any semblance of foreign control. Dr. Sun Yat-sen and General Huan Hsing both declared against foreign supervision.

On June 18, the Shanghai Chinese Chamber of Commerce took the novel step of requesting the British Minister of Foreign Affairs to persuade the syndicate to modify the more stringent terms of the proposed loan. Sir Edward Grey's reply, communicated through His Majesty's Minister at Peking, was as follows:[40] " Sir Edward Grey has authorized me to inform the Chamber of Commerce in reply that so far the action of the groups has met with the entire approval of His Majesty's Government, who, however, cannot urge the Banks to make any loan which does not, in their opinion, offer adequate guarantees for the proper and useful expenditure of the proceeds and satisfactory security for the payment of principal and interest; and further, that in regard to all questions connected with this loan His Majesty's Government is acting, and will continue to act, in full accord with the other governments concerned."

The protraction of the loan negotiations had the result that several provinces, being in desperate financial straits, negotiated independent loans with certain foreign commercial houses, as for instance, the firms of Skoda, Diederichsen, and Krupp, in return for large contracts for arms and ammunition. Various other expedients were adopted by the Central Government, all of which while relieving a temporary necessity merely increased the difficulties of an already almost hopeless

[40] See " China Year Book," 1913, page 357.

financial problem. Finally the Chinese Minister of Finance decided to negotiate with the representatives of an independent British Syndicate, which appeared at that time on the Chinese financial market, for a larger loan of L10,000,000. On July 12th a preliminary agreement and on August 30th the final contract for what became known as the Crisp loan was signed in London. The contract contained among others the following provisions: [41]

" Article IV. The payments of interest and the repayments of the principal of the loan and all other amounts required for or incident to the service of the loan shall be and hereby are constituted a first charge on the surplus revenues of the Salt Gabelle, the total annual revenue of which amounts to Forty-seven Million Five Hundred and Ten Thousand Kuping Taels, of which Twenty-four Million Taels per annum are already hypothecated. The remaining Salt Revenue is hereby declared to be free from all loans, liens, charges, or mortgages.

" Article VII. The price of the bonds to the Chinese Government shall be eighty-nine per cent. of their nominal value.

" Article IX. The rate of interest for the loan shall be five per cent. gold per annum on the nominal principal. . . . The term of this loan and of the bonds evi-

[41] See " China Year Book," 1913, page 360.

dencing the same shall be forty years from the date issue of the loan to the public.

" Article XIV.   The Chinese Government engages not to issue nor to authorize the issue of any other external loan until the whole of this loan has been issued to the public . . . but if the Chinese Government should desire to obtain further foreign capital before this loan is realized, and the terms offered by the Financial Group are as favorable as those offered by others, preference shall be given to the Financial Group."

This latter article and the hypothecation of the surplus revenues of the Salt Gabelle as well as the absence of any effective control provisions were considered highly detrimental to the interests not only of the Sextuple Syndicate but also of the Chinese Government.   Therefore, as soon as the conclusion of this agreement became known the Sextuple Group refused to comply with the request of the minister of finance for further advances, while the British minister at once informed the Chinese Government that his government did not approve of the new loan and warned China that her policy was liable to alienate the powers principally interested in her finances.   The British Foreign Office had previously been approached by Mr. Crisp with the view of soliciting the British Government's support in his proposed loan.   The Foreign Office's refusal and attitude is explained in a telegram from Sir Edward Grey to Sir J.

Jordan of August 23rd:[42] " It was explained to Mr.
Crisp that, as a matter of general principle, His Majesty's
Government would never support a loan concluded
without adequate guarantees for the control of the
expenditure of the proceeds and without proper security.
The fact that the Six Power Consortium, with the full
support of the respective governments, had so far been
unable to obtain satisfactory terms in these respects from
the Chinese Government, rendered it very improbable
that a syndicate without the same experience and un-
supported by any foreign government could meet with
a greater success."

After the refusal of the international syndicate to
make the advances requested the Chinese Government
decided to avail itself of at least half of the sum offered
by Mr. Crisp and L5,000,000 were issued in London
shortly afterward. But the Chinese minister of finance
made it at the same time understood " that China desired
to deal with the six groups as the only combination
capable of furnishing within the next few years the
enormous sums which China would need to reorganize
her administration and finance the industrial development upon which the Peking Government wished to em-
bark."[43] For this reason, the Chinese Government
finally induced Mr. Crisp to agree to the cancellation

[42] See " China," No. 2, 1912, Vol. CXXI, No. 22.
[43] See Straight, op. cit., page 147.

of Article XIV, as demanded by the Group, and of the
flotation of the second half of his loan in return for
L150,000 compensation.[44]

The international loan negotiations were continued
and an early signature of the Reorganization Loan agreement was expected on all sides, when, early in 1913 new
obstacles arose, which again threatened to wreck the
negotiations. The source of the difficulty was this time
certain Foreign Powers who, actuated by selfish motives,
and in a highly discreditable manner began to scramble
about the appointment of Foreign Adviser. It had been
understood that China intended to nominate a Dane to
the position of Chief Inspector of the Salt Administration and that a German would be nominated Director
of the National Loans Department. The only appointment about which there was any uncertainty was that
of the Adviser to the Accounts and Audit Department.[45]
But when the list of names was submitted to the Foreign
Legations, the French and Russian legations formally
objected to a scheme which included advisers of neutral
nationality as well as a German. A suggestion then was
made that two advisers of Russian and French nationality respectively be appointed for the Audit Bureau,
the American and Japanese ministers disclaiming any
ambitions for advisorship.

[44] See " China Year Book," 1914, page 379.
[45] See " China Year Book," 1914, page 381.

The decision to make nationality the chief qualification for the adviserships was open to many objections from the Chinese point of view, particular exception being taken to the appointment of a Russian at a time when diplomatic relations were so seriously strained by the Mongolian situation. Matters were therefore again brought to a complete deadlock.

It was during this deadlock that President Wilson, in a reply to a communication from the American group, announced that the administration had refused the request of the group to sanction American participation in the loan. The eventual resumption of serious negotiations with what had then become the Quintuple Syndicate was probably due in no small measure to the fact that it was brought to the attention of the Chinese Government that under an old loan contract the Russian Government could claim the appointment of an adviser as a treaty right.[46] China ultimately agreed to appoint the foreign advisers as proposed by the foreign minister, while the banks on their part agreed to rearrange the price of the loan and to reduce the rate of interest from 5½ to 5 per cent.

The Reorganization Loan Agreement was finally signed at Peking on the twenty-sixth day of April, 1913, between the government of the Republic of China of the one part, and the Hongkong and Shanghai Banking

[46] See "China Year Book," 1914, page 383.

Corporation, The Deutsch-Asiatische Bank, The Banque de l'Indo-Chine, The Russo-Asiatic Bank, and The Yokohama Specie Bank of the other part.[47] The amount was 25,000,000 pounds sterling at 5 per cent. per annum. "In reimbursement of expenses connected with the payment of interest and with the repayment of principal of the loan the Banks are hereby granted by the Chinese Government a Commission of one-fourth per cent. on the annual loan service." (Article X.) "The price of this present loan or of any series thereof to the Chinese Government shall be the price of its issue to the public on the London market less a deduction by the Banks of six per cent. of the nominal value of the bonds, the issue price in London to be not less than ninety per cent., securing to China a net price of not less than eighty-four per cent. for the entire loan. The Banks shall be responsible for all expenses connected with the issue of the loan." (Article XIII.) "The term of the loan shall be forty-seven years." (Article IX.) According to Article IV — "This entire loan, together with any advances which may be made in connection therewith, is hereby secured in respect to both principal and interest by a charge upon the entire revenues of the Salt Administration of China, subject to previous loans and obligations already charged on the security thereof and not yet redeemed, as detailed in the statement

[47] For text see "China Year Book," 1914, pages 387 ff.

attached to this Agreement, and it shall have priority both as regards principal and interest over all future loans, charges and mortgages charged upon the abovementioned revenues so long as this loan or any part thereof shall be unredeemed. No loan, charge or mortgage shall be raised or created which shall take precedence of or be on an equality with this loan, or which shall in any manner lessen or impair its security over the said revenues of the Salt Administration of China, so far as required for the annual service of this loan, and any future loan, charge or mortgage shall be made subject to this loan, and it shall be so expressed in every agreement for any such future loan, charge or mortgage."

International "control" is established through the following provisions: "Article V.— The Chinese Government engages to take immediate steps for the reorganization with the assistance of foreigners of the system of collection of the salt revenues of China assigned as security for this loan, in the manner which has been determined upon by the Ministry of Finance and which is as follows: — The Chinese Government will establish a Central Salt Administration at Peking, under the control of the Minister of Finance. This Central Salt Administration will comprise a Chief Inspectorate of Salt Revenues under a Chinese Chief Inspector and a foreign Associate Chief Inspector, who will constitute the chief authority for the superintendence of the issue of licenses and the compilation of reports and returns of revenues. In each salt producing district there will be a branch office of the Chief Inspectorate, under one Chinese and one foreign district inspector who shall be jointly responsible for the collection and deposit of the salt revenues. The engagement and dismissal of these Chinese and foreign district inspectors, and of the necessary Chinese and foreign staff at the chief and branch inspectorates, will be decided jointly by the Chinese and foreign chief inspectors, with the approval of the Minister of Finance. . . .

" Release of salt against payment of dues in any district will be made only under joint signature of the Chinese and foreign district inspectors, the revenues so collected to be lodged by them in a ' Chinese Government Salt Revenue Account ' with the banks or with depositories approved by the banks, and reported to the Chief Inspectorate for comparison with their returns. This Salt Revenue Account shall be drawn upon only under the joint signatures of the Chief Inspectors, whose duty it will be to protect the priority of the several obligations secured upon the salt revenues.

" So long as the interest and principal of this loan are regularly paid there shall be no interference with the Salt Administration as herein provided, but if interest and/or principal be in default at due date, then after a reasonable period of grace the said organization shall forthwith be incorporated with the Maritime Customs and the revenues above pledged shall be administered for the account and in the interest of the bondholders."

An Audit Department under foreign supervision is established in Article XIV: " The Chinese Government engages at once to put into effective operation an Account and Audit Department, under the Provisional Regulations Promulgated by a Presidential Order dated the 15th of November, 1912, and published in the *Official Gazette* of November 16th, 1912, copy and translation of which are hereto attached in Annex H of this agreement, subject to the understanding that any modifications which may be found necessary shall not impair their effect in regard to this loan.

" The Chinese and foreign directors of the Bureau of National Loans shall witness their approval of all requisitions for loan funds by their joint signatures thereon.   Withdrawals of loan funds from the banks shall be for amounts corresponding to the actual requirements of disbursements.

" Cheques and/or orders upon the banks for the withdrawal of loan funds shall be signed by a duly authorized representative of the Minister of Finance and shall be sent, together with the supporting requisitions duly signed as above, and the relative ' orders to pay ' to a representative of the banks to be designated.   The said representative of the banks, after satisfying himself that the expenditure is in accordance with Article II of this agreement and the annexes therein referred to, shall forthwith countersign the cheque and return it to the Ministry of Finance for representation to and payment by the banks.

" Should the said representative of the banks be in doubt in respect to disbursements of loan funds which have been made, he shall be entitled to make inquiries of the foreign director of the Bureau of National Loans and to call upon him for the production of receipts and vouchers for inspection."

The terms agreed upon were substantially those demanded by the bankers at the beginning of the negotiations. The conclusion of the loan was followed by widespread political agitation. Both the Senate and the House of Representatives returned the government's dispatch announcing the conclusion of the loan and requesting its registration. Dr. Sun took the extreme step of telegraphing to the governments and peoples of the foreign powers denouncing the loan as a highhanded and unconstitutional matter.

The government had a hard stand in defending its attitude and action. The minister of finance and the president drew the attention of the country to the fact, that foreign nations had pressed for payment of outstanding foreign loan charges. The following dispatch from the Provisional President was sent to the Senate on May 7, 1913:[48] "Further delay of payment would evoke forcible interference in the administration of our national taxes which served as securities to the various loans. Then foreign supervision of our finance would actually begin and the Republic would be in danger of bankruptcy. . . . The loan was an absolute necessity." In a telegram from Tutuh Po, according to the minister of finance, it was stated:[49] "There will be foreign supervision if you borrow, but there will also be foreign supervision if you do not borrow. Therefore it would be more advisable to undergo temporary suffering; so that there may be a resurrection from that death."

The government's policy was backed by the merchant class, disinterested patriots and the older officials, who were in favor of a large loan being raised for purposes of reorganization and economic development. These parties,— as opposed by the loudly patriotic press, the students and ambitious politicians who perceived that foreign control meant the curtailment of their opportunities — recognized at the same time the necessity of foreign control. This is Mr. Bland's opinion, who informs us that, " the merchants of the Treaty Ports, and, generally speaking, the classes that have a stake in the country, are . . . in favor of expert supervision and

48 See " Far Eastern Review," Vol. 9, page 531.
49 See " China Year Book," 1914, page 386.

honest handling of foreign loans, recognizing the fact
that only by these means can the money be spent to the
country's economic advantage." [50]

The absolute necessity of a large loan might, perhaps,
best be illustrated by an enumeration of the purposes
for which the net proceeds of the loan were to be used.
Over half of them were for the repayment of debts,
while the administration expenses of the Central Government (to cover a deficit in the regular budget), the
disbandment of troops of various provinces, and the
reorganization of the Salt Gabelle only claim a smaller
portion of uses. The respective figures are stated in
the appendices of the Loan Agreement thus: [51]

A.	Liabilities due by the Chinese Government: (Including Arrears of Boxer Indemnity, repayment of advances, Treasury Bills, Interest and Sinking Fund of previous loans)	L 4,317,778
B.	Provincial Loans:	2,870,000
C.	Liabilities of the Chinese Government shortly maturing:	3,592,263
D.	Disbandment of Troops:	3,000,000
E.	Current Expenses of Administration: (Estimated from April to Sept., 1913)	5,500,000
F.	Reorganization of the Salt Administration:	2,000,000
	Total	L 21,280,041

If taken at the minimum figure of 84 per cent. the net
proceeds of the loan would still leave a deficit of L280,-
041. To these requirements of the Chinese Government

[50] See Bland, op. cit., page 394.
[51] See "China Year Book," 1914, pages 397 ff.

then should be added the sum of L7,000,000 for currency
reform — considering that the currency loan of 1911
has not been floated — L3,000,000 for Manchurian
industrial development and many more millions for the
eighteen provinces for industrial development and administrative reform. The financial requirements of China
in 1912 were set forth in an article in the *North China
Herald* of Sept. 28, of which we give the following
abstract: " It is necessary to state . . . that the merchants, banks, and other rich Chinese who helped the
new government, both during the struggle and after,
now stand badly crippled from want of funds. They
have been often told that their outstandings would be
cleared as soon as the first loan with the foreigner was
closed. Trade is badly in need of the funds spent on
the revolution. . . . The amount on this score is not
available, but the lowest estimate puts it at about taels
20,000,000. . . . It would seem that if foreign loans
should serve any beneficial purpose at all for China, a
sum of L40,000,000 is necessary during the year ending,
say next June; and further amounts, into the details
of which it is too early now to go, appear likely to be
needed in the coming years." And further: " There
is no doubting that any syndicate proposing to lend
money to China should be able to arrange for L40,000,-
000 during the next nine months, and be able to pay
about L60,000,000 during the next three years. The

original proposal of the sextuple group was arranged on this basis, and the total of L60,000,000 was agreed upon as necessary for the regeneration of the country. . . . That the banks composing the sextuple group, with their respective governments at their back, would be able to supply China with this large total with more facility than any number of other syndicates is beyond question. The Chinese themselves know it, and hence their anxiety to keep on good terms with the group in spite of their latest action."

The banks composing the syndicate were not only able but also willing to supply China with all the money she needed — provided her credit could be maintained. But China's credit can only be maintained by preventing indiscriminate borrowing and wasteful expenditure and by enhancing the value of the securities upon which her credit rests. In order to maintain China's credit the bankers felt it would be absolutely necessary for their financial agents to have a certain advisory capacity during the contract and a supervision over the revenues upon which their bonds were secured — last not least so as to place Chinese bonds at a price that would maintain China's credit as well as the confidence of the bondholders. Those who have criticized the attitude of the syndicate, have, as Mr. Straight points out, " in a measure lost sight of some of the elementary functions of a banking house which handles foreign loans. They have forgotten that it is not the bankers themselves who provide the money to finance a foreign loan, though they may for a time advance from their own resources certain preliminary payments. Bond issues, however, are sold to the public, the bankers receiving their commission on the sale, and the reputation of a house of issue like that of any other commercial establishment depends upon the quality of the commodity which it sells. Bankers would not be justified in requesting their clients to take bonds on a sentimental and not a business basis any more than the president of an insurance company would be warranted in loaning funds for which he was responsible to a personal friend regarding whose solvency he had no guarantee. . . . The groups have not been attempting to force money, with humiliating conditions attached, on China. They have stated merely that they are willing, only upon certain conditions, to loan the money which China has requested them to furnish. The groups do not insist that China accept a loan if these conditions are unacceptable. They do say that they will not issue Chinese bonds on terms which they regard as unsatisfactory." [52]

The position of China's credit in 1912 was highly unsatisfactory, for China had neither sufficient nor stable security for the amount that it was necessary for her to borrow. It was therefore imperative to build up

[52] See Straight, op. cit., pages 155 and 157,

the revenues in order to provide a margin for future borrowing. The most important security that China could offer for the repayment of, and interest upon, any extensive foreign loans which were required for reorganization purposes was, by verdict both of foreign and Chinese financiers, the Salt Gabelle. Foreign loans involving an annual charge of about 27,000,000 taels were in 1913 already secured upon this revenue. To this sum were to be added 12,500,000 taels, constituting the annual interest upon the 25 million Pound Sterling Reorganization Loan, not considering, however, repayments of principal which were to begin after the eleventh year. Considering that the total revenue from salt hitherto had been approximately 40,000,000 taels per annum,[53] there was no margin left for further loans, while the maintenance of this figure was by no means assured.

The reform of the salt revenue system, since 1913, has at least equaled any reasonable expectation. A few figures have established a glorious vindication for a reasonable financial " control." The results of the salt tax for 1914 proved to be $58,826,000; the revenue of 1915 was $69,000,000; and the figure of the salt tax revenue in the Budget of 1916 is $84,771,365.[54]

As in the old days the credit of the Chinese Government was built upon the foreign controlled International

[53] See " China Year Book," 1915, page 310.
[54] See " China Year Book," 1916, page 320.

Maritime Customs Service, so has China's credit to-day been materially enhanced through the reorganization of the Salt Gabelle under international control. That advantages have accrued to China as well as to the world from this form of control is beyond doubt.

CHAPTER IX

CONCLUSION

It was the purpose of the preceding chapters to analyze the problem of foreign control in China, formulated in the introduction, on a scientific basis. It need hardly be said that any formulation in the field of international relations is, in the present period of transition, liable to undergo material alterations, although it will, of course, always retain a historical value. This point seems so clear that it would require no further illustration and comment if it were not for the fact that the struggle of international forces in China presents a problem of such stupendous difficulties and possibilities for new complications as to make the value of a formulation doubly questionable. In way of conclusion then, we shall enlarge and comment upon certain important aspects of the problem which it has been impossible for us fully to explain within the limits of the preceding chapters, and which, besides, it was not strictly within the purposes of the present work closely to discuss.

Things had previous to the world war reached a pass in which every power was pledged to every other power to uphold the integrity of China, the open door, and equal opportunity. But at the same time the very national existence of China was at stake. We have seen Northern and Southern Manchuria parceled off and trespassers warned away, Outer Mongolia alienated, Inner Mongolia threatened, and Shantung, Fukien, the Yangtsze Valley and the Southwest Provinces reserved for special exploitation. All that aggrandizement, disguised under some railway loan and properly called a "conquest by railroad and bank," was primarily incited by the natural pressure of financial and industrial forces seeking expansion from the constricted confines of the stronger, more advanced and over-populated manufacturing countries — although it cannot be denied that one or two of the powers had motives of a purely political character.

Foreign commercial pressure was nothing new to the Chinese. In fact it had been exercised, only in a different form, for almost a century. Under great pressure the Chinese were first prevailed upon to open up a certain number of their ports as points of contact between themselves and the outside world. As soon as a foothold in the treaty ports was gained, began the process of seizing territory. The powers were always demanding more privileges of intercourse until of late years they started this determined and concerted campaign for spheres of interest and railway concessions. The foreigners were eager to build railroads, not because they thought the Chinese needed the railroads but because the foreigners needed the profit of the railroads. This then is a point of supreme significance, namely: that the bottom idea of all the treaty stipulations and agreements as to intercourse, customs, extraterritoriality, spheres of interest, railway concessions and control was not the welfare of the people of China, but the profit and ease of doing business by the people of the West. With the exception of a few missionaries and a few scholars, writers and artists who admire Chinese civilization, the interest of the world was a money interest pure and simple.

That the motive of foreigners was money-making — or land-stealing — the Chinese have fully discovered from an intercourse of over a hundred years. They had also discovered that under the régime of extraterritoriality, of international settlements, leased territories, concessions, railway zones and control of Chinese sovereignty and Chinese rights were disregarded at innumerable times and they found that the interests of China were never consulted, although she had to pay the bills. These bills consisted of an unfavorable balance of trade and a heavy foreign debt, which threatened to result in bankruptcy and the control of China by foreign governments acting for their citizens. China's financial distress had mainly arisen from the burden of indemnities exacted by foreigners and from an increase of ex-

penditures incurred to gain the power of defense against
the foreigner. The obvious and natural way of over-
coming these financial difficulties would have been for
China to increase her exports over her imports, or at
least to increase the quantity of commodities required
to be exported to maintain a commercial equilibrium.
But in fact the tendency has been in the direction of an
increase of imports. China has never been a creditor
nation due to the fact that the foreigner insisted upon
supplying the Chinese with goods which they did not
want by creating an artificial demand for them, while
China had nothing much to export that the foreigner
stood in need of. The heavy excess of imports of merchandise over exports was finally met to some degree by
sales of large blocks of railway stocks and bonds which
should thus prove another source of usefulness to the
foreigner.

For all these reasons the Chinese showed an obstinate
determination to keep the foreigner out or to treat him
with watchful seclusion and to obstruct his designs
wherever he had to be admitted, or to revolt openly
against him. Indeed the Chinese as a nation have always wished to be left alone; they did not desire the
presence of the foreigner; and any interference, even for
their good, was resented by them. It was resented in
an unmistakable manner; for the Chinese have an extraordinary capacity for passive resistance. Says Sar-

gent: [1] " The Chinese may be coerced into restraining their resentment for a time; the history of their relations with European powers proves amply that they neither change nor forget. Once they obtain sufficient material force, they are likely to assert, in no uncertain fashion, the claim to that right enjoyed even by minor Western nations, the right to determine for themselves the conditions of intercourse with foreigners. The vast possibilities of the country suggest the thought that the consequences, whether political or economic, may not redound to the advantage of the Western nations which have hitherto treated China as an uncivilized region, to be exploited for the sole benefit of the self-elected exponents of the ideas and methods of European civilization."

China's foreign policy has been stable and decided. By dint of intellectual force and superior diplomatic tactics the Chinese have usually overcome the most serious conditions. And in unmistakable terms have they given the world to understand that they will not be friendly with an alien race which either usurps their government or assumes a dictatorial attitude towards it, or tries to exploit the country and its inhabitants:— until the West woke up and took stock of the Chinese people and began to reëstimate its strength of resistance and its potential power. Whereupon it dawned upon

[1] See Sargent, op. cit., page 309.

the world that the Chinese are anything but a decadent or exhausted race; on the contrary, that they possess many qualities that go to the making of a strong and efficient people.

For these and other reasons which we shall mention presently, the foreign powers gradually moderated their ambitions with a view of an ultimate abandonment of the spheres of interest policy and a redeclaration to the adherence of the " Open Door " doctrine in its widest sense. They began to realize that further international jealousies, than which there could be nothing more pernicious to their individual interests, could only be avoided through an internationalization of Chinese finance and an international participation in any great money transaction. With such internationalization of railways and loans was to be combined an internationalization of financial control. Only thus could the foreign powers hope to enforce their terms — which was fully understood by Count Hayashi, when he wrote:[2] " The attitude of the powers towards China has of recent years undergone considerable change. This has put their acting in unison quite within the limits of possibility. Nowadays political considerations are of minor importance, as compared with economic considerations. . . . There is no longer any desire to obtain control of parts of China, for China is a very difficult country to manage

[2] See Hayashi, op. cit., pages 302 and 307.

and the population is very large." Or again: "The way to deal with China is for the powers to combine and insist on what they want and to go on insisting until they get it. . . . Here are only these alternatives before the powers. They must either bring their combined forces to bear on China to get what they want or else leave her alone, until like an awakened lion she is ready to spring on her prey, in which case she will be powerful enough to threaten the acquired rights of all the powers."

Notwithstanding any possible political advantages of international coöperation in China, it cannot be doubted that the principal reasons underlying it were of a purely economic character. The financial world had, before the outbreak of the war, begun to consider the conception of nations as hostile competitors in world finance as one economically unsound. The new and growing tendencies of a genuinely international finance tended towards elimination of competition and towards consolidation and substitution of pacific motives. As the economic standardization of the world proceeded, the coöperation of the financiers of the various countries in business enterprises in all parts of the world began to bind up the prosperity of each individual country intimately with the welfare of all other countries. Says Hobson, [3] "Modern finance is the great sympathetic system in an economic organism in which political divisions are of

[3] See Hobson, "Investment," page 122.

constantly diminishing importance. That which Christianity, justice, and humane sentiment have been impotent to accomplish through nineteen centuries of amiable effort, the consolidation of financial interests, through bourses, loans, companies, and the other machinery of investment, seems likely within a generation or two to bring to consummation, namely, the provision of such a measure of effective international government as shall render wars between civilized powers in the future virtually impossible."

In spite, or rather, in consequence, of the present war this principle of concerted action in finance and diplomacy will be no passing phase. In a survey of the future it is apparent that nations, at least certain nations, will become more rather than less connected, and as such will often find it advantageous to pursue identical lines of policy, especially in Oriental countries. If the world is to be given a chance for anything like a permanent settlement at the conclusion of this war, the watchword will have to be "international coöperation," certainly not international economic strife. The construction of railways and administrative loans by an international syndicate then probably represents one line to which events point for the Chinese problem, which still ranks as the greatest capitalistic proposition of the near future. Such coöperation will simultaneously have the inherent merit of being "a guarantee for the preservation, rather than an instrument for the destruction, of China's integrity," as Mr. Straight says.[4] For our investigation will have it made obvious, that, when a balance of interests exists among the powers, China can come out of great trouble with less damage than has been the case in the era of exclusive spheres of interest.

This latter point is of importance in view of the fact that a measure of foreign financial control in some form or another has become as essential to China's preservation as the borrowing of foreign capital. International intercourse is as dependent upon legalized relationships as is domestic intercourse upon the preservation of law and order. But the insecurity of former times has not been remedied much by the new Republican régime. That, because the revolution was by no means a revolution of the Chinese people or of Chinese institutions, but merely the accidental triumph of a body of politicians mainly due to the treason of Yuan Shih-Kai. The instincts and traditions of Asiatic races cannot be suddenly changed by the drafting of a constitution. To quote Bland: "Destitute of constructive genius, without authoritative leaders or permanent elements of cohesion, the Chinese Republic has been suddenly conferred upon a people that neither wants nor understands representative government." [5] The Chinaman as a factor in public

---

[4] See Straight, op. cit., page 120.
[5] See Bland, op. cit., page 147.

CONCLUSION 279

life as the West conceives the idea is as yet an unknown quantity. The nation, as a whole, does not concern itself with political affairs any more than, on the advice of Confucius, it concerns itself with theological affairs. To illustrate this: it has been estimated that less than 5 per cent. of the population were really concerned in the overthrow of the monarchy.[6]

There will be no hasty transformation of scene in China, which would be as disastrous to her as an over-investment of capital. China's hope lies not in a sudden revolutionary destruction of the old order, but in slow, steady growth, by educative processes, which shall enable the nation to adapt itself gradually to its changed environment. Only in a very small degree have the Chinese begun to realize the idea of nationality, of a central government, of a uniform legal system, and of taxation as distinguished from tribute and official perquisites. Left now to work out her own salvation on these and other lines, China's progress would be painfully slow and surely harmful to foreign interests: — therefore the necessity of a mild and friendly form of international financial " control," at least in such matters as affect the foreigner directly; of which our Chapter VIII served as illustration.

The advisability of international financial coöperation and control being established, there remains for discus-

[6] See Whelpley, op. cit., page 270.

sion only the all important question, whether such coöperation will be possible. If Japan is prepared to fall in with an international scheme it will no doubt stand a good chance of being carried out. And the cordial relations now existing between Japan, the United States, Great Britain, and France lend color to the assumption that there will henceforth be financial coöperation in China, at least among these four powers. Such financial coöperation would certainly not conflict with Japan's Eastern Asiatic Doctrine. For the latter aims, as does the Monroe Doctrine in the Americas, at a political, not at an economic, exclusion of Western Powers.

However, the future is too uncertain even for any trustworthy formulation of the new problems which are just shaping in the Far East. But whatever the future may hold in store, it seems clear that we must first adopt a generous, tolerant spirit of mutual respect, if we hope at all to further the cause of international good relations in the Far East. To use the words of Professor Brown: [7] " Our task becomes one of determining the specific mutual interests which nations are prepared to recognize; and then to endeavor, in a spirit of toleration, friendly concern, and scientific open-mindedness, to formulate the legal rights and obligations which these interests entail.

[7] Brown, " International Realities," page 226.

" The great preliminary work of facilitating closer relations, of removing misunderstandings, of reconciling conflicting points of view, of identifying various interests, of fostering common conceptions of rights and obligations remains yet to be done."

An absolutely unbiased contribution to such preliminary work was our task.

BIBLIOGRAPHY

I. Official Documents:

France:
Documents Diplomatiques (Livres jaunes).
Rapports Commerciaux des agents diplomatiques et consulaires du France.

Germany:
Der Reichsanzeiger.
Das Staatsarchiv.

Great Britain:
British and Foreign State Papers.
Diplomatic and Consular Reports.
Parliamentary Papers (Blue Books).
(Referred to as "China.")

United States:
Diplomatic Correspondence of the United States.
Executive and Legislative Documents of the United States.
Foreign Relations of the United States.
United States Consular Reports.

II. Collections of Treaties:

American Journal of International Law, Supplements to.
Hertslet, E. Sir, Treaties Between Great Britain and China and Between China and Foreign Powers, 3rd edition, revised, London, 1908.
Martens, G. F. de, Nouveau Recueil Général de Traités.
Malloy, W. M., Treaties Between United States and Other Powers, Washington, 1910.
Mayers, W. F., Treaties Between the Empire of China and Foreign Powers, Shanghai, 1897.
Rockhill, W. W., Treaties and Conventions with or Concerning China, 1894–1904, Washington, 1904.
See also: British and Foreign State Papers.

III. The China Year Book, 1912, 1913, 1914.

IV. Periodicals, etc.:

L'Asie Française.
The Far Eastern Review.

The Journal of the American Asiatic Association. Now "Asia."
The London Times, Daily and Weekly.
The North China Herald.
Der Ostasiatische Lloyd.

V. Theory of International Relations:
Bastable, C. F., The Theory of International Trade, London, 1913.
Brown, P. M., International Realities, New York, 1917.
Hall, W. E., International Law, Oxford, 1909.
Harms, B., Volkswirtschaft und Weltwirtschaft, Jena, 1912.
Hobson, C. K., The Export of Capital, London, 1914.
Hobson, J. A., An Economic Interpretation of Investment, London, 1911.
Hobson, J. A., International Trade, London, 1904.
Hobson, J. A., Work and Wealth, Chapter XVII, New York, 1914.
Köbner, O., Kolonialpolitik, Jena, 1908.
Leroy Beaulieu, P., De La Colonisation, Paris, 1908.
Liszt, F. Von, Das Völkerrecht, Berlin, 1907.
Oppenheim, L., International Law, London, 1905.
Reinsch, P. S., World Politics, New York, 1902.
Reinsch, P. S., Colonial Government, New York, 1906.
Withers, J. F., International Finance, London and New York, 1916.

VI. Literature referring to the whole thesis as well as to Chapters I and II:
Bland, J. O. P., Recent Events and Present Policies in China, London, 1012.
Bland, J. O. P., and Blackhouse, China Under the Empress Dowager, London, 1910.
Boulger, D. C., History of China, London, 1898.
Brinkley, F., China, 4 vols., Boston, 1902.
Colquhoun, A., China in Transformation, New York, 1912.
Colquhoun, A., English Policy in the Far East, London, 1885.
Cordier, H., Histoire des Relations de la Chine avec les Puissances Occidentales, 3 vols., Paris, 1902.
Curzon, G., Problems of the Far East, Westminster, 1896.
Douglas, R. K., Europe and the Far East, Cambridge, 1913.
Harrison, J., Peace or War East of Baikal? Shanghai, 1910.
Hazen, C. D., Europe Since 1815, New York, 1910.
Hornbeck, S. K., Contemporary Politics in the Far East, New York, 1916.

Hsu, M. C., Railway Problems in China, Columbia University
Studies, New York, 1915.
Ireland, A., China and the Powers, Boston, 1902.
Kent, P. H., Railway Enterprise in China, London, 1907.
Krausse, A., The Far East, London, 1900.
Laboulaye, E. de, Les Chemins de Fer de Chine, Paris, 1911.
Lawton, Lancelot, The Empires of the Far East, Boston, 1912.
Leroy Beaulieu, P., The Awakening of the East, New York,
1900.
Mahan, A. T., The Problem of Asia and Its Effects upon
International Policies, Boston, 1900.
Millard, T., Our Eastern Question, New York, 1916.
Morse, H. B., The International Relations of the Chinese
Empire, London, 1910.
Morse, H. B., The Trade and Administration of China, Lon-
don, 1913.
Okakura, K., Ideals of the East, London, 1903.
Reinsch, P. S., Intellectual and Political Currents in the Far
East, Boston, 1911.
Sargent, A. J., Anglo-Chinese Commerce and Diplomacy, Ox-
ford, 1907.
Schüler, W., Abriss der Neueren Geschichte Chinas, Berlin,
1913.
Schumacher, H., Die Organisation des Fremhandels in China,
Leipzig, 1911.
Staunton, Sir G., The Englishman in China, etc., Edinburgh
and London, 1900.
Wagel, G. R., Finance in China, Shanghai, 1915.
Weale, B. L. P., The Re-Shaping of the Far East, New York,
1905.
Weale, B. L. P., The Truce in the East and Its Aftermath,
New York, 1907.
Weale, B. L. P., The Coming Struggle in Eastern Asia, Lon-
don, 1908.
Williams, S. W., Anson Burlingame, New York, 1902.

VII. Special Literature referring to Chapter III:

Alexinsky, Gregor, Russia and the Great War, London, 1915.
Beveridge, A. J., The Russian Advance, New York, 1903.
Cahen, G., Histoire des Relations de la Russie avec la Chine,
etc., Paris, 1912.
Carruthers, D., Unknown Mongolia, London, 1914.
Gerrare, W., Greater Russia, New York, 1903.
Golder, F. A., Russian Expansion on the Pacific, Cleveland,
1914.

286   BIBLIOGRAPHY

Krahmer, G., Russland in Ostasien, Leipzig, 1904.
Krausse, A., Russia in Asia, Leipzig, 1899.
Mavor, J., An Economic History of Russia, Toronto, 1914.
Ravenstein, E. G., The Russians on the Amur, London, 1861.
Ular, A., A Russo-Chinese Empire, Westminster, 1904.
"Vladimir" Russia on the Pacific, etc., London, 1899.
Weale, B. L. P., Manchu and Muscovite, London, 1904.

VIII. Special Literature referring to Chapter IV:
Antonini, P., L'Annan, le Tonkin et l'Intervention de la
    France, Paris, 1899.
Billot, M., L'Affaire du Tonkin, Paris, 1888.
Doumer, P., L'Indo-Chine Française, Paris, 1905.
Dubois, M., et A. Ferrier, Les Colonies Françaises Chapitre
    VIII, L'Indo-Chine Française, Paris, 1902.
Grandmaison, L. D., L'Expansion Française au Tonkin, Paris,
    1898.
Leroy Beaulieu, P., De la Colonisation, Vol. II, Chapter XI.

IX. Special Literature referring to Chapter V:
Franke, O., Deutschland und England in Ostasien, Hamburg,
    1914.
Franke, O., Deutschland und China, etc., Hamburg, 1914.
Mackey, B. L., China, Die Republik der Mitte, Stuttgart, 1914.
Riesser, J., Die Deutschen Grossbanken, Jena, 1900.
Rohrbach, P., und von Dewall, Deutschland und China nach
    dem Kriege, Berlin, 1915.
Wertheimer, F., Deutschland und Ostasien, Stuttgart, 1914.

X. Special Literature referring to Chapter VI:
Asakawa, K., The Russo-Japanese Conflict, Westminster,
    1904.
Aubert, L., Paix Japonaise, Paris, 1906.
Autremer, J. D., The Japanese Empire, London, 1910.
Dyer, H., Dai Nippon, London, 1904.
Gulick, G. L., Evolution of the Japanese, New York, 1904.
Hishida, S. C., Japan as a Great Power, Columbia Studies,
    New York, 1905.
Longford, J. H., Japan of the Japanese, London, 1911.
Masaoka, N., Japan's Message to America.
Murdoch, J. and Yamagata, A History of Japan, 2 vols., Yo-
    kohama, 1903-10.
Okuma, Count, Fifty Years of New Japan, 2 vols., London,
    1909.

Pooley, A. M., The Secret Memoirs of Count Hayashi, New York, 1915.
Porter, R. P., The Full Recognition of Japan, London, 1911.
Saito, Hisho, A History of Japan, London, 1912.
Stead, A., Japan by the Japanese, New York, 1904.
Suyematsu, K., The Risen Sun, New York, 1905.

XI. Special Literature referring to Chapter VII:
Abbott, James Francis, Japanese Expansion and American Policies, New York, 1916.
Foster, J. W., A Century of American Diplomacy, Boston, 1900.
Foster, J. W., American Diplomacy in the Orient, Boston, 1903.
Fox, Frank, Problems of the Pacific, Boston, 1912.
Kawakami, K., American-Japanese Relations, New York, 1912.
Leroy-Beaulieu, P., Les États Unis, le Japon et la Russie dans le Nord du Celeste Empire. Economiste français, 1910.
Millard, T. F., America and the Far Eastern Question, New York, 1909.

XII. Special Literature referring to Chapter VIII:
McCormack, F., America and the Chinese Loan, Scribners, Vol. 50, page 349.
McCormack, F., How America got into Manchuria, Century, Vol. 81, page 622.
Straight, Willard, China's Loan Negotiations, in Clark University Addresses, 1912, New York, 1913.
Winston, A. P., Chinese Finance Under the Republic, Quarterly Journal of Economics, Vol. XXX, Aug., 1916.

INDEX

THE END

AMERICAN BUSINESS ABROAD

Origins and Development
of the Multinational Corporation

An Arno Press Collection

Abrahams, Paul Philip. *The Foreign Expansion of American Finance and its Relationship to the Foreign Economic Policies of the United States, 1907-1921.* 1976

Adams, Frederick Upham. *Conquest of the Tropics:* The Story of the Creative Enterprises Conducted by the United Fruit Company. 1914

Arnold, Dean Alexander. *American Economic Enterprises in Korea, 1895-1939.* 1976

Bain, H. Foster and Thomas Thornton Read. *Ores and Industry in South America.* 1934

Brewster, Kingman, Jr. *Antitrust and American Business Abroad.* 1958

Callis, Helmut G. *Foreign Capital in Southeast Asia.* 1942

Crowther, Samuel. *The Romance and Rise of the American Tropics.* 1929

Davids, Jules. *American Political and Economic Penetration of Mexico, 1877-1920.* 1976

Davies, Robert Bruce. *Peacefully Working to Conquer the World:* Singer Sewing Machines in Foreign Markets, 1854-1920. 1976

de la Torre, Jose R., Jr. *Exports of Manufactured Goods from Developing Countries.* 1976

Dunn, Robert W. *American Foreign Investments.* 1926

Dunning, John H. *American Investment in British Manufacturing Industry.* 1958

Edelberg, Guillermo S. *The Procurement Practices of the Mexican Affiliates of Selected United States Automobile Firms.* 1976

Edwards, Corwin. *Economic and Political Aspects of International Cartels.* 1944

Elliott, William Yandell, Elizabeth S. May, J.W.F. Rowe, Alex Skelton, Donald H. Wallace. *International Control in the Non-Ferrous Metals.* 1937

Estimates of United States Direct Foreign Investment, 1929-1943 and 1947. 1976

Eysenbach, Mary Locke. *American Manufactured Exports, 1879-1914.* 1976

Gates, Theodore R., assisted by Fabian Linden. *Production Costs Here and Abroad.* 1958

Gordon, Wendell C. *The Expropriation of Foreign-Owned Property in Mexico.* 1941

Hufbauer, G. C. and F. M. Adler. *Overseas Manufacturing Investment and the Balance of Payments.* 1968

Lewis, Cleona, assisted by Karl T. Schlotterbeck. *America's Stake in International Investments.* 1938

McKenzie, F[red] A. *The American Invaders.* 1902

Moore, John Robert. *The Impact of Foreign Direct Investment on an Underdeveloped Economy: The Venezuelan Case.* 1976

National Planning Association. *The Creole Petroleum Corporation in Venezuela.* 1955

National Planning Association. *The Firestone Operations in Liberia.* 1956

National Planning Association. *The General Electric Company in Brazil.* 1961

National Planning Association. *Stanvac in Indonesia.* 1957

National Planning Association. *The United Fruit Company in Latin America.* 1958

Nordyke, James W. *International Finance and New York.* 1976

O'Connor, Harvey. *The Guggenheims.* 1937

Overlach, T[heodore] W. *Foreign Financial Control in China.* 1919

Pamphlets on American Business Abroad. 1976

Phelps, Clyde William. *The Foreign Expansion of American Banks.* 1927

Porter, Robert P. *Industrial Cuba.* 1899

Queen, George Sherman. *The United States and the Material Advance in Russia, 1881-1906.* 1976

Rippy, J. Fred. *The Capitalists and Colombia.* 1931

Southard, Frank A., Jr. *American Industry in Europe.* 1931

Staley, Eugene. *Raw Materials in Peace and War.* 1937

Statistics on American Business Abroad, 1950-1975. 1976

Stern, Siegfried. *The United States in International Banking.* 1952

U.S. Congress. House of Representatives. Committee on Foreign Affairs. *The Overseas Private Investment Corporation.* 1973

U.S. Congress. Senate. Special Committee Investigating Petroleum Resources. *American Petroleum Interests in Foreign Countries.* 1946

U.S. Dept. of Commerce. Office of Business Economics. *U.S. Business Investments in Foreign Countries.* 1960

U.S. Dept. of Commerce. Office of Business Economics. *U.S. Investments in the Latin American Economy.* [1957]

U.S. Dept. of Commerce and Labor. *Report of the Commissioner of Corporations on the Petroleum Industry:* Part III, Foreign Trade. 1909

U.S. Federal Trade Commission. *The International Petroleum Cartel.* 1952

Vanderlip, Frank A. *The American "Commercial Invasion" of Europe.* 1902

Winkler, Max. *Foreign Bonds, an Autopsy:* A Study of Defaults and Repudiations of Government Obligations. 1933

Yeoman, Wayne A. *Selection of Production Processes for the Manufacturing Subsidiaries of U.S.-Based Multinational Corporations.* 1976

Yudin, Elinor Barry. *Human Capital Migration, Direct Investment and the Transfer of Technology:* An Examination of Americans Privately Employed Overseas. 1976